Make that Grade
Human Resource
Management

THIRD EDITION

Linda Reidy

Gill & Macmillan

137542

Gill & Macmillan Ltd
Hume Avenue
Park West
Dublin 12
with associated companies throughout the world
www.gillmacmillan.ie

© 2003, 2007, 2011 Linda Reidy
978 07171 5006 9
Print origination in Ireland by Carole Lynch
Printed by GraphyCems, Spain

The paper used in this book is made from the wood pulp of managed forests. For every tree felled, at least one tree is planted, thereby renewing natural resources.

A catalogue record is available for this book from the British Library.

For Eoin

TO THE READER

This book was written as a revision text for students of human resource management (HRM). To ensure that you **understand** and **remember** what you read, you are encouraged to actively participate in your learning process. You will understand and retain the information better if you follow this advice:

Read the **objectives** sections at the start of each chapter carefully. They provide a structure for the whole chapter and help you to focus on the material as you read it. When you have finished the chapter, look back at the objectives and make sure that you have achieved them.

In most of the chapters you will find **exercises** for you to complete. Do not skip over these exercises, as they have been designed to help you to:

- concentrate on what you are reading
- make connections between theory and practice
- remember what you have learned

Write down the answers to these questions as you go along. It is important that you learn to express yourself in words before you take your exams. If you have difficulty writing the answers having just read the material, think of how much more difficult it will be to write them in an exam.

Towards the end of each chapter you will find a list of the **important terms and concepts** used. Make sure you understand what each one means as well as the context in which it was used.

Write answers to the **revision questions** which you will find at the end of each chapter. Answer in as much detail as possible, making sure that you keep to the point.

You are strongly encouraged to **further research** the topics covered in this book. This is a revision text, designed to cover the main functions of HRM. For further information, look up some of the references at the back of the book as well as the websites mentioned in chapters nine, ten and eleven.

CONTENTS

SECTION 1

INTRODUCTION TO HRM

Chapter 1 Introduction to Human Resource Management

What is human resource management?
Is it the same as personnel management?
What factors affect how HR operates in an organisation?
What kind of work is done in the HR department?
How can HRM operate in organisations?
What are the current challenges for HR practitioners?

Section one provides some answers to these questions.

1
INTRODUCTION TO HUMAN RESOURCE MANAGEMENT

Objectives

This chapter will help you to:
- define human resource management (HRM)
- become familiar with the concept of HRM and its place in an organisation
- trace the historical development of HRM
- explain the theoretical differences between personnel management and human resource management
- discuss the context within which HR operates
- identify the nature of work done in HR departments
- outline how models of HRM can be applied in organisations
- discuss the current HR challenges facing organisations

Definition

Human resource management (HRM) is a style of managing people in the workplace that emerged during the 1980s. It is defined by Armstrong (2006, p.3) as 'a strategic and coherent approach to the management of an organisation's most valued assets – the people working there who individually and collectively contribute to the achievement of its objectives'.

The term 'strategic approach' is a key phrase in the definition of human resource management and signifies the importance of a long-term 'game plan' for employing and managing people at work.

Armstrong (1999, p.3) says that HRM 'is concerned with the employment, development and reward of people in organisations and the conduct of relationships between management and the workforce'.

The functions of the HR department, which involve employing, developing and rewarding workers as well as employment relations, form the focus of the rest of this book.

Two approaches to HRM can be identified. **'Hard' HRM** treats people just like any other resource to be managed effectively. The emphasis of this approach is on organisational needs rather than the needs of employees. The **'Soft' HRM** approach recognises that because people think and feel, they cannot be treated in the same way as other resources. The focus is on nurturing and developing staff as a means of achieving corporate aims.

The Evolution of HRM

This section outlines how the style of managing people has evolved over time. It will help you to understand how the role of the human resource manager has developed over the past two hundred years.

The evolution of HRM will be discussed under the following headings:
1   The origins of HRM
2   The influence of scientific management
3   The influence of behavioural science
4   Changes in people and organisations

> As you read, try to concentrate on how the role of the HR manager has been shaped into what it is today.

1 The origins of HRM

Managing people at work began at the time of the **industrial revolution** in the late eighteenth century. Before this time few large organisations existed, but, with the invention of new technology, the factory system developed and large numbers of people moved into the towns and cities to work. The work environment was very unfavourable at this time and employees, including young children, worked very long hours for very little pay in difficult and often dangerous working conditions. The approach to managing people was harsh and the main aim was to control the workers who had few, if any, rights. Some of Charles Dickens' novels, such as *Hard Times*, depict the lives of the working class of this era.

The first efforts to show concern for workers came toward the end of the nineteenth century when some large organisations decided to improve the situation of their employees. Companies such as Cadbury in Britain and Jacob in Ireland appointed **welfare officers** to improve working conditions and to set up schemes for sick pay and subsidised housing. This initiative was voluntary as the companies did not have any legal obligations to provide these benefits for their employees. Even though the welfare approach suffered setbacks during times of economic recession, the concern for the welfare of workers is still an important part of HR management today. This is reflected in the role of the HR manager in drawing up organisational policies on harassment and sick pay, for example. Evidence of the progress made for workers can be seen in the employment legislation regarding equality, dismissal, young workers, minimum pay and health and safety. Today's HR managers must keep up to date with these legal developments to ensure that their organisation meets its obligations to employees.

2 The influence of scientific management

The next influence on how people were managed was '**scientific management**', which became popular early in the twentieth century. In an effort to organise the work process more efficiently, FW Taylor asserted that there was 'one best way' to approach every job. To find the best way of doing a particular job, Taylor analysed the job and broke it down into individual components. This is called job specialisation. Taylor believed that people could be trained to become expert at one particular component of the job. Companies like Ford took up Taylor's ideas at the time and used assembly lines to complete the job bit by bit. Taylor's ideas can be seen at work in some fast-food restaurants where the process of serving a customer is broken down into a number of tasks and each employee is responsible for one of these tasks, such as taking the customer's order, frying burgers or cooking fries. While scientific management can improve efficiency, it ignores the fact that people are not machines and they can get bored doing the same thing all the time. HRM today still benefits from some of the tools developed during this time. These include job analysis, methods of selection and methods of training.

3 The influence of behavioural science

The research of people like Elton Mayo in the 1930s and 1940s indicated that the way people felt about their jobs influenced how they did their work. For the first time it was acknowledged that performance could be affected by concepts such as motivation, job satisfaction, group dynamics and leadership style. The main contribution of the **behavioural science movement** to HRM is the knowledge gained from research in these and other areas. Those involved in managing people now have to consider how individual differences among employees affect the management style required. People are different in terms of what they expect from their jobs and how committed, satisfied and motivated they are, and may need to be treated differently. This requires a more flexible approach from managers.

4 Changes in people and organisations

During the 1980s and 1990s, a time of worldwide recession, many business leaders recognised that their employees were the key to competitive advantage. This belief, that people are a resource to be managed as efficiently and effectively as any other resource, led to a shift in management style which became known as **human resource management**.

This development in management style has certainly been influenced by the fact that both the workers and the organisations which employ them have changed considerably over the last two hundred years. The standard of education has increased and employees expect better working conditions and better treatment from employers. Furthermore, today's workers are more likely to take an interest in the performance of their organisation and often want to be involved in the decision-making that directly affects them.

Organisations have changed too. Due to technological developments, change occurs more quickly now, and an organisation has to be able to adapt to the changing environment in order to survive. An organisation's ability to adapt to change relies heavily on its employees.

This view of the employee as a valuable resource led to the emergence of new theories of how people should be managed. There are a number of theoretical differences between this new style of HRM and the traditional approach of personnel management. The next section looks at these in more detail.

> Before you read the next section, make sure you understand what you have just read. Can you explain the factors that have influenced the role of the HR manager today? Use the four subheadings above to structure your answer.

Theoretical Differences between Personnel Management and HRM

In theory, HRM is not a synonym for personnel management. Instead it should be viewed as another perspective on managing people. The key word in the title of this section is 'theoretical'. This is because in reality the 'personnel' and 'HR' titles do not always reflect the style of management dominant in the organisation. In other words, just because an organisation has a personnel manager, it does not necessarily follow that the old style of management is used. Similarly, just because an organisation employs an HR manager, it does not mean that HR policies and strategies are evident in the organisation. There are a number of key areas where differences in these styles of management can be identified.

The following differences will be discussed:

1 Integration
2 Strategy
3 Management–employee relations
4 Organisational design

As you read this section, think about the style of managing people in an organisation you are familiar with.

Which style of management most closely resembles that of your organisation?

Overall, does the organisation lean towards the traditional personnel style of management or towards HRM?

---

1 Integration

Where 'personnel' is the dominant style of management, almost all of the responsibility for the personnel management role is taken on by the personnel specialist, that is the personnel officer or the personnel manager. In contrast, the human resource role is integrated. In other words, HR activities are present in all areas and are carried out at all levels of the organisation. This requires the involvement of line managers in developing HR strategies and carrying out HR policies. In organisations which lean towards the HR style of managing people, responsibility for planning, selection, training, discipline and other aspects of personnel management do not lie solely with the HR manager.

In addition to the integration between business and HR strategies, there should be integration among the HR activities themselves. In other words, HR practices should be compatible. For example, if employees are required to work in teams, then rewards should be designed to remunerate effective teamwork.

Using a **competency-based approach** to managing people is an example of how key HR activities can be integrated. By clearly identifying the competencies (the skills, knowledge and personal attributes) necessary to attain high levels of performance, a competency framework can be established and applied to other aspects of HR management, such as:

- planning – to form part of the job analysis (see chapter two)
- selection – to aid the choice of selection methods and to formulate relevant interview questions (see chapter four)
- training and development – to focus on specific competencies (see chapter five)

- appraisal – to evaluate employees' performance (see chapter six)
- reward management – to decide how much employees should be paid (see chapter eight)

2 Strategy

A key characteristic of organisations that adopt the HR style of management is that a strategy for human resources is included in the overall corporate strategy. This means that plans for recruiting, developing and motivating employees are viewed as an important part of the long-term planning of the organisation. Human resource management involves the development of long-term plans and strategies with regard to these and other aspects of managing people. The HRM approach is proactive as it tries to anticipate problems and situations before they happen. Traditional personnel management planning tends to be short-term and may be more reactive in nature. This means waiting for problems to occur before solutions are sought.

3 Management–employee relations

Personnel management is based on the pluralist view that workers and management have different and conflicting interests. For example, workers would like to increase pay as much as possible and employers would like to increase profits as much as possible. This implies that there is low trust between workers and management. If this is the case, the members of each group need to protect their own interests by joining unions or employer associations. Employment relations can be adversarial and this affects how pay and conditions are negotiated. Those in unionised workplaces rely on collective bargaining to agree on these issues and the outcome is the same for everybody. This style of management focuses on compliance. In other words, managers concentrate on ensuring that employees keep their end of the bargain by following rules and procedures.

In contrast, human resource management is identified as being a unitarist approach. This is the assumption that workers and management have the same goals within the organisation. It implies that there is no conflict of interest between workers and management. If this is the situation, there should be a high level of trust between workers and management and this eliminates the need for union protection. Individual bargaining is encouraged, meaning that each worker negotiates their own contract. HR managers believe that this style of management will lead to more than just compliance. The aim is to increase commitment so that workers feel a sense of loyalty and responsibility to the organisation. For this to happen, good employment relations are necessary.

4 Organisational design

Organisational design refers to the overall structure of an organisation and includes the interaction of elements such as the definition of roles, the allocation of responsibilities, job design and the distribution of power. There tend to be some differences in the design of organisations that follow the traditional personnel management style and those that apply the strategies of human resource management. Personnel management is more likely to be found in bureaucratic organisations with strict job descriptions and clearly defined roles. Human resource management is more likely to be found in organic organisations where flexibility in work roles is encouraged. This means that workers may be expected to fill in for each other if necessary or take on duties outside of their area of responsibility if the need arises. Power and decision-making tend to be centralised in one individual or a few individuals in organisations where the personnel management style dominates. In contrast, these responsibilities are more likely to be shared or devolved in organisations where HRM is the main management style.

It is important to point out that one style of management is not necessarily better than the other. Rather one style of management may be more appropriate in a particular type of organisation.

Can you remember the key differences between the two styles of management? Read through the section again and underline all the key words which can be used to distinguish between personnel and human resource management. Make a list and compare it with table 1.1 in the summary section of this chapter.

The Context within which HRM Operates

In practice, there is great variation among organisations in their approach to managing workers. This variation is due to the contexts or environments in which organisations operate. In other words, how people are managed at work depends on circumstances both inside and outside the organisation. HR strategy, policies, procedures and practices are influenced by factors such as the economy, the labour market, social issues, technology and legislation as well as the organisation's objectives, culture and size.

The economy

The economic situation can affect an organisation in several ways. It can have an impact on salary trends and on demand for goods and services. In times of economic prosperity, HR practitioners may need to design strategies to attract and retain employees. During a downturn in the economy, the strategic focus may shift to downsizing and reducing the workforce.

The labour market

The condition of the labour market is another important factor. For instance, if there are large numbers of qualified people available for work, the organisation is under less pressure to formulate recruitment plans or to invest in training and development. This was the situation for many Irish companies in the late 1980s and early 1990s and again in the late 2000s and early 2010s. When suitably qualified personnel are scarce, they become more valuable to the organisation and are treated accordingly. A shortage of qualified nurses in Ireland in the early 2000s, for example, resulted in some hospitals recruiting nurses from abroad and offering more flexible hours in an effort to fill vacancies.

Social factors

The demographic changes in the Irish population have led to the development of policies on, for example, diversity, work-life balance and flexible working to accommodate the specific needs of groups of workers such as women, students, people from different countries and people with disabilities. Consumer lifestyles and attitudes to social and environmental issues also affect demand for an organisation's products or services.

The technological context

Developments in technology have changed the environment within which HR operates. Communication within organisations is facilitated by the use of email and intranet. Vacancies can be advertised and applications processed online. In addition, HR software is now widely used to carry out basic administrative tasks such as storing employee profiles and recording absences. A self-service option allows employees to access their own records, view their pay history and update personal details.

The legal context

Employment legislation is another component of the environment in which HRM operates. Laws on health and safety, dismissal, maternity and equality are examples of the legal influences on the management of human resources and affect areas such as recruitment, selection and termination of employment. Employers have certain legal obligations to their employees and these have some bearing on management style. Employment legislation is discussed in more detail in chapter eleven.

Organisation's objectives

An organisation's objectives, as specified within its corporate strategy, provide part of the context within which it operates. For example, if an objective is to expand the business or to launch a new product, HR activities may focus on hiring new staff or on providing training to sales staff.

Organisation's culture

An organisation's culture also influences how HRM works in the organisation. Organisational culture refers to the accepted way of doing things within a place of work. If the culture traditionally encouraged compliance with procedures and discouraged initiative, it is difficult to make a sudden change to a culture of commitment and participation. An organisation's culture develops gradually over time and can be hard to change quickly. For this reason new organisations can more easily adopt the characteristics of the HRM style than older ones.

Organisation's size

The size of an organisation can affect how people are managed. For example, relations between employees and management in smaller companies tend to be less formal and there is less likely to be union representation. This can make it easier for smaller organisations to adopt some of the ideas and principles of HRM. Contracts are often negotiated on an individual basis in smaller organisations, whereas larger ones have to apply the same policies and strategies to all their employees. Union representation, common in larger organisations, underlines the notion that workers and management have different agendas. Thus, the principles of HRM are more difficult to integrate into a larger organisation.

How does an organisation you know respond to each of the factors discussed in this section? Discuss how these factors may influence HR strategy and practice.

The HR Department

This section of the chapter takes a brief look at the kind of work carried out by people employed in human resources. There are four main areas of responsibility:
- employee resourcing
- employee management
- employment relations
- record-keeping

The **employee resourcing** process involves making sure that the organisation has the right number of employees with the appropriate skills and qualifications. This process needs to be reviewed continuously and is aided by HR planning, recruitment and selection (see chapters two, three and four).

Employee management is the area of responsibility that covers human resource development, performance appraisal, motivating employees and reward management (see chapters five, six, seven and eight).

The human resource department also has a role to play in **employment relations**. Trade unions and employers' associations, dispute resolution facilities and employment legislation are discussed in the last section (see chapters nine, ten, and eleven).

A very important aspect of the work of HR practitioners is **record-keeping**. In some cases record-keeping is a specific requirement of employment legislation. Annual leave, rest breaks and payment of wages, for instance, must be documented and employers may be penalised for not retaining accurate records. Records of grievance and disciplinary issues and of performance appraisals should also be kept in case it is necessary to defend a claim from an employee. Several HR software products are available to record, store and retrieve HR information.

Models of HRM

Models of how human resource management can be used in organisations fall into two categories: '**best practice**' and '**best fit**'.

Best practice models assume that there is one best way to carry out HR functions and that this way can be applied to all organisations. Well-known examples of best practice models are those of Pfeffer (1998) and Guest (1989, 1997).

Jeffrey Pfeffer proposes that the components of best practice HRM are:

- employment security and internal labour markets
- selective hiring and sophisticated selection
- extensive training, learning and development
- employee involvement, information sharing and worker voice
- self-managed teams/teamworking
- high compensation contingent on performance
- reduction of status differentials/harmonisation

> To what extent does an organisation you are familiar with follow the components of best practice outlined by Pfeffer?

Figure 1.1 *Guest's model of HRM*

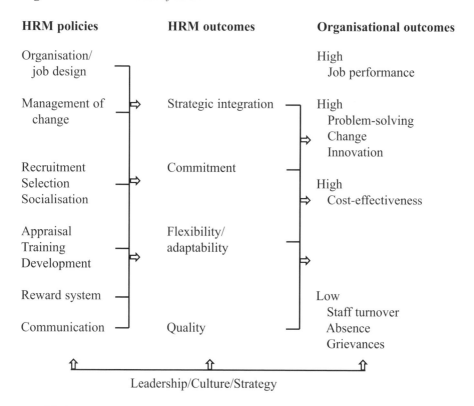

David Guest, Professor of Organisational Psychology and Human Resource Management at King's College London, developed a model of how human resource management can work in organisations. According to this model, organisations will be more successful if they aim to achieve four key HRM goals. These goals are:

- **strategic integration** – the organisation should aim to integrate human resource management with its overall business strategy
- **commitment** – the organisation should encourage employee commitment. This is the extent to which an individual identifies with and is involved in the organisation
- **flexibility** – the organisation should aim for flexibility both in the content of jobs and in the structure of the organisation
- **quality** – the organisation should aim for high standards of quality in the work that is carried out, the people that are employed and the treatment of employees by management

These four goals can be achieved through careful consideration of how jobs will be designed, how change will be managed and how recruitment and selection will be carried out, for example (see the first column of figure 1.1). If all four HRM goals are achieved, the organisation can expect the benefits listed in the third column under the heading 'Organisational outcomes'. These include better performance and problem-solving and lower staff turnover and absenteeism. Guest believes appropriate leadership, strategic vision and culture are necessary for HRM to be effective.

What are Guest's four goals of HRM, how can they be achieved and what are the benefits to the organisation of achieving these goals?

Best fit models are based on the belief that there is no 'one best way' to manage human resources and that HR policies and practices depend on the internal and external environment in which the organisation operates. Examples include the **Business Life-Cycle Model** and the **Competitive Advantage Model**.

The Business Life-Cycle Model proposes that the approach to HRM depends on which stage of the business life cycle (see figure 1.2) the organisation is at.

At the **start-up stage** of a new organisation, the HR focus tends to be on recruitment, retention, flexibility and gaining employee commitment. Usually there are few formalised HR practices at this stage.

At the **growth stage**, formal policies and procedures are needed and can be based on early experience. More sophisticated methods of recruitment, selection, development and so on may be used. Motivation, retention and morale become more important.

At the **maturity stage**, there is likely to be a range of formalised HR procedures. There may be a focus on the control of labour costs. As a result, relationships may become tense between employees/unions and employers.

At the **decline/renewal stage**, the emphasis may shift to redundancy. HR policies are reconsidered and training may focus on reskilling.

Figure 1.2 *Business life cycle*

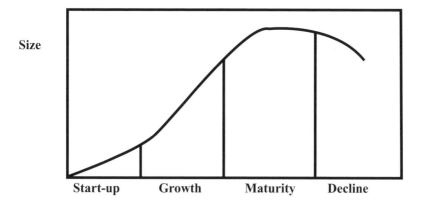

BUSINESS LIFE CYCLE

Think about an organisation you know. What stage of the business life cycle is it at currently? How has this influenced HR practices?

Porter (1985) argues that employers have three basic strategic options in order to gain **competitive advantage**: cost reduction, quality enhancement and innovation.

The **cost reduction** employer seeks to produce goods and services that are cheaper than the competition and puts an emphasis on minimising costs at all stages of the process. Likely HR implications include low levels of pay, tight performance monitoring, poor or non-existent training and no unions.

The **quality enhancement** employer seeks to produce goods and services of the highest quality possible in order to stand out from the competition. The likely HR implications are similar to those of the best practice models, namely systematic recruitment and selection, comprehensive induction programmes, highly competitive pay and benefits and a partnership approach to employment relations.

The **innovation** strategy to competitive advantage involves groups of highly trained specialists who work closely together to design and produce complex and rapidly changing products and services. Common HR implications include a greater emphasis on informality, problem-solving groups and flexibility. In addition, dynamic reward systems and individual bargaining are common practice.

> Can you think of any organisations that match these strategies for competitive advantage? How do these strategies for competitive advantage affect HR practices in the organisations you have identified?

Current HR Challenges Facing Organisations

During the economic boom, one of the biggest difficulties facing HR managers was **attracting and retaining key employees**. Many employers found it difficult to fill vacancies. HR practitioners focused on recruitment and reward strategies in an effort to ensure adequate staffing levels. The situation has changed dramatically in the last few years, however. While attracting and retaining key employees remains a problem for some organisations, the economic recession has forced many others either to downsize their operations or to close them completely, resulting in a **surplus of staff**. One of the main challenges currently facing HR practitioners, therefore, is deciding the best way to deal with employees who are no longer required. Possibilities include offering career breaks, redeployment, reduced working hours, layoffs, job sharing and redundancy.

The composition of the labour market is changing in Ireland, as in other countries, with an increased number of women, non-Irish, older workers and members of minority groups entering the labour market. Despite the existence of the Employment Equality Acts (1998–2008) (see chapter eleven), the Equality Authority (see chapter ten) received 731 referrals in 2009. The majority of the casework activity was based on the grounds of age, race, gender and disability. The challenge for HR practitioners, and indeed all managers, is to work within the law in order to **manage diversity** in the workplace fairly and effectively.

The needs of organisations and employees can be met by increased **flexibility** on both sides. The use of flexitime, home-working, job sharing and flexible job descriptions are examples of how flexibility can benefit both employees and the organisation. Work-life balance initiatives and family-friendly policies can help to attract and retain employees as well as address some of the issues in managing diversity and dealing with surplus staff.

Employees nowadays are likely to want to be involved in organisational decision-making. **Employee participation**, in the form of quality circles, attitude surveys and teamworking for example, allows employees to contribute to decision-making in the organisation. The 'partnership approach' is based on the idea that cooperative bargaining can benefit all parties involved and has been used at national level in Ireland to negotiate national pay agreements.

Central to each of the HR issues confronting employers is the challenge of **managing change**. Organisational change is inevitable, but is likely to be met with resistance from either employers or employees. See Kotter and Schlesinger (1979) for a discussion on strategies for overcoming resistance to change.

Working within the law is a constant challenge for employers today. From advertising a vacancy through to termination of employment, employers need to know what their legal obligations are towards employees. Employment legislation is discussed in more detail in chapter eleven.

Summary

This chapter began with a definition of HRM and an outline of the main factors that influenced the management of people over time:
• the origins of HRM
• scientific management
• behavioural science
• changes in people and organisations

The next section discussed the theoretical differences between personnel and human resource management. Table 1.1 outlines the key words used to describe each style of management.

Table 1.1 *Theoretical differences between personnel management and HRM*

	Personnel	HRM
Integration	low (specialist roles)	high (integrated roles)
Strategy	short-term planning reactive	long-term strategy proactive
Relations	pluralist low trust collective bargaining compliance	unitarist high trust individual bargaining commitment

Organisational design	bureaucratic
	defined work roles
	centralised power and
	    decision-making
		organic
		flexibility in work roles
		shared power and
		    decision-making

The section on theoretical differences was followed by a discussion of the context within which HRM operates. The factors outlined were:

- the economy
- the labour market
- social issues
- technology
- legislation
- organisation's objectives
- organisation's culture
- organisation's size

The next section gave an overview of HR work carried out in organisations. The main areas outlined were:

- employee resourcing
- employee management
- employment relations
- record-keeping

A distinction was made between 'best practice' and 'best fit' models of HRM and four models of how HRM can operate within an organisation were summarised:

- Pfeffer
- Guest
- business life cycle
- competitive advantage

Finally, current HR challenges facing organisations were raised. These included:

- attracting and retaining key employees
- dealing with surplus staff
- managing diversity
- issues of flexibility
- employee participation
- managing change
- working within the law

Important Terms and Concepts

attracting employees	labour market
behavioural science	managing change
best fit	organisational design
best practice	participation
business life cycle	partnership approach
commitment	pluralist
competency-based approach	quality
competitive adavantage	retaining employees
compliance	scientific management
diversity	'soft' HRM
flexibility	strategy
'hard' HRM	surplus of staff
integration	unitarist

Revision Questions

1 Discuss the evolution of human resource management, focusing on the influences that have shaped the current role of the HR manager.
2 Analyse the theoretical differences between personnel and human resource management.
3 Discuss the factors that influence how HRM works in an organisation.
4 Outline the nature of work carried out in HR departments.
5 Distinguish between 'best practice' and 'best fit' approaches to HRM.
6 Outline how the models of HRM can be used in an organisation.
7 Discuss the HR challenges that currently face organisations in Ireland.

SECTION 2

THE EMPLOYEE RESOURCING PROCESS

Chapter 2 Human Resource Planning
Chapter 3 Recruitment: Attracting Candidates to the Organisation
Chapter 4 Selection: Choosing the Right Person for the Job

How can an organisation prepare for future staffing requirements?
How can it attract and select the right people?

One of the functions of HRM is to implement and monitor complementary processes which will ensure that the organisation obtains and retains the people it needs to achieve organisational goals. These processes are described in this section.

2
HUMAN RESOURCE PLANNING

Objectives

This chapter will help you to:
- define human resource planning
- explain the importance of human resource planning
- identify human resource planning as part of the overall organisational strategy
- examine current human resources in an organisation
- describe the main components of a job analysis
- forecast demand and supply of labour
- devise, implement, review and evaluate HR plans
- examine how the human resource planning process works

Definition

Human resource planning is an ongoing examination of the number and type of employees required by an organisation and leads to the formulation of strategies designed to help the organisation to achieve its goals.

Beardwell and Claydon (2007, p.158) define human resource planning as 'the process for identifying an organisation's current and future human resource requirements, developing and implementing plans to meet these requirements and monitoring their overall effectiveness'.

Before you read the next section, think about why planning human resources is so important.
Why is it useful for the organisation to plan ahead for its human resource needs?

The Importance of HR Planning

In chapter one it was noted that long-term strategic planning is one of the distinguishing characteristics of human resource management. Human resource planning is of major importance because the organisation needs to be prepared as far as possible for changes in its internal and external environments. HR planning helps to prepare the organisation to deal with future staff and skill requirements so that it can achieve its **strategic objectives**. The success of the organisation's goals for increasing market share, increasing production or developing new products depends on having the right number of employees with the appropriate skills and qualifications when they are required. Poor HR planning can be costly for an organisation, for example in terms of work lost due to staff shortages. Information acquired through planning provides the foundation of HR strategies which help the organisation to achieve its objectives by:

- avoiding staff shortages
- anticipating a surplus of employees
- identifying skills shortages
- specifying training needs
- aiding the selection of suitable employees
- preparing the organisation for change
- attempting to meet both employee and organisational expectations within the workplace

HR Planning as Part of the Overall Organisational Strategy

HR planning is an essential part of the overall **corporate strategy**. Planning for human resources cannot be carried out satisfactorily without consultation with line managers and reference to the organisation's strategic plan. This is because making decisions on whether to recruit or train employees depends on organisational plans, such as whether a new product will be launched or new technology introduced. Conversely, devising organisational plans should involve discussion with human resource planners to ensure the availability of suitable employees. The remainder of this chapter examines the process of HR planning.

The HR Planning Process

This section describes the four stages in the HR planning process.

Before you read on, look at figure 2.1 and think about how each of the four stages might be carried out.

Figure 2.1 *The process of human resource planning*

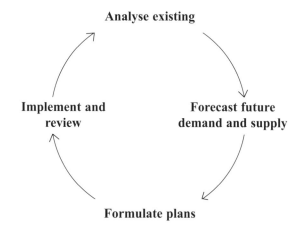

Imagine you are involved in HR planning in an organisation you are familiar with. As you read, concentrate on how the following information could be useful.

Analysis of the existing situation

Before the organisation plans ahead for its staffing and skill requirements, it is important to examine the current situation. This involves an examination of:

1 The organisation's internal environment
2 The organisation's external environment

1 The internal environment

Examination of the **internal environment** can be accomplished by:

• developing an employee profile or **employee database**
• carrying out a **job analysis**

Assessing current human resources begins by compiling a **profile** of the organisation's employees. This is sometimes called 'stocktaking'. Just as the retailer keeps a record of every item in stock in the shop at a particular time, a profile of each employee should be compiled. Information is gathered from CVs, performance appraisals and forms completed by employees specifically for this purpose. The final inventory should include a complete list of employees by:

- name
- age
- qualifications
- prior employment
- specialised skills
- performance ratings
- length of service

In terms of strategic human resource planning, such a **database** is a valuable tool for assessing the skills currently available in the organisation. Managers may not be aware that employees possess skills other than those necessary to carry out the jobs they were employed to do. The information gathered is also useful for decision-making with regard to the selection of individuals for training, promotion and transfer as well as the development of recruitment plans.

Job analysis is a systematic analysis of jobs within an organisation. A job analysis is carried out to identify the human behaviour necessary for adequate job performance. It is divided into three parts and involves describing the job in detail, specifying the kind of person required to do it and outlining the terms and conditions of the job.

The components of a job analysis are:

- job description
- person specification or competency framework
- terms and conditions

The **job description** forms the basis for the contract of employment. The main elements are:

- job title
- who the employee reports to
- who reports to the employee
- who the employee liaises or works with
- main tasks
- responsibilities

Figure 2.2 *Sample basic job description*

Title:	Trainee manager
Dept:	Grocery
Reports to:	Grocery manager
Responsible for:	Sales assistants
Main tasks:	• supervising staff • working with suppliers • dealing with customers • any other duties as directed by manager

The **person specification** outlines the skills and experience necessary to carry out the tasks and responsibilities of the job. It provides details of the type of person the organisation wishes to employ. The person specification should match the job description and include details of the following:

- qualifications
- knowledge
- specific skills and aptitudes
- experience
- personal attributes

Figure 2.3 *Sample person specification*

Job title:	Trainee manager	
Dept:	Grocery	
Job requirements	**Essential**	**Desirable**
Education	Cert. in Business Studies	HRM as a component of course
Experience	1 year's work experience in retail	Experience in grocery dept
Skills	Good interpersonal skills	Computer literate

The person specification is often based on classifications such as **Rodger's Seven-Point Plan** (Rodger, 1952):

1 Physical make-up – health, physique, appearance, bearing and speech
2 Attainments – education, qualifications, experience
3 General intelligence – fundamental intellectual capacity
4 Special aptitudes – mechanical, manual dexterity, facility in the use of words or figures

5 Interests – intellectual, practical, constructional, physically active, social, artistic

6 Disposition – acceptability, influence over others, steadiness, dependability, self-reliance

7 Circumstances – domestic circumstances, occupation of family

The extent to which these characteristics are essential or desirable should be specified.

An alternative to the person specification is the use of **competency frameworks**. Competencies are 'all the work-related personal attributes, knowledge, skills and values that a person draws upon to do their work well', as defined by Roberts (1997). Instead of designing a person specification for each job, it may be possible to draw up a framework of competencies that can be applied to all of the jobs within an organisation. The Irish Civil Service has adopted this approach and has identified seventeen competencies, some of which are listed below:

- communication skills
- customer service
- analytical abilities
- teamwork
- initiative
- leadership skills

Use of the competency-based approach provides an opportunity to integrate HR activities, as the competencies identified can be applied in processes such as recruitment, selection, training and in the design of payment systems.

Examples of **terms and conditions** which should be explained are:

- details of hours to be worked
- holidays
- payment
- fringe benefits (such as health insurance, pension plan)

When producing the documentation described above, the organisation's obligations with regard to **equal opportunities legislation** must be considered. Care must be taken not to discriminate against anyone because of age, sex, marital status, race, religion or sexual preference or because they are a member of the Travelling community. For more detailed coverage of equality legislation, see chapter eleven.

The job analysis is carried out by collecting information in a number of ways. These include:

- interviewing job-holders to get details of how jobs are completed
- observing how employees carry out their work
- having workers complete questionnaires designed for the purpose of job analysis
- asking employees to keep job diaries
- having discussions with managers and supervisors

> Using the Internet and/or other resources, search for job descriptions and person specifications for jobs that you are interested in.

The information provided by a job analysis is useful to the organisation for:

- HR planning
- recruitment and selection decisions
- identification of training needs
- job design
- performance appraisal
- job evaluation

2 The external environment

The development of both an employee profile and a job analysis involves the assessment of the situation within the organisation. HR planners also need to keep up to date with developments outside the organisation that may have an impact on the organisation's requirements for human resources. You may remember that some aspects of the organisation's external environment were discussed briefly in chapter one in relation to the context within which HR operates. Knowledge of the **labour market**, the **economic situation** and current **employment legislation** is necessary for human resource planning. In addition, it is important to keep abreast of developments in technology that might affect the organisation.

Beardwell and Holden (1997) propose that this analysis of the current environment leads to the development of:

- recruitment plans – to avoid unexpected staff shortages
- training plans – to avoid skill shortages
- management development plans – to avoid managerial shortages or to avoid bottlenecks in the system
- industrial relations plans – to avoid industrial unrest resulting from changes in the quantity or quality of employees

Forecasting demand and supply of labour

Once the organisation has a clear idea of the human resources currently available, it is necessary to prepare a forecast of future staff and skill shortages and surpluses. In other words, the organisation must estimate whether it will need to increase or decrease the number or type of employees over the coming weeks and months. Predicting future human resource needs is difficult in the long term. For example, it would have been impossible for organisations to predict the 'volcanic ash cloud' and the effect it would have in April 2010. Flights were cancelled but airlines still had to pay employees even if they were not working, whereas ferry companies had to find extra staff at short notice to meet the increased demand for their services. As is the case with the weather, short-term staffing forecasts are more accurate than long-term ones.

In order to prepare a human resource forecast, two aspects of the future situation need to be considered. First, the organisation needs to estimate the future quantity and quality of people required, that is the future **demand for labour**. In addition, it must measure the number of people likely to be available within and outside the organisation, in other words the **supply of labour**. These will be discussed separately.

Demand for labour

Demand for labour is estimated after considering:
- managerial judgement
- business plans
- past trends
- modelling techniques

Successful planning largely depends on the **experience** and **judgement** of the manager in trying to predict the number and type of employees that will be needed in the future, and when exactly they will be required.

Examination of the organisation's **future plans** aids the calculation of future demand for labour. The organisation's corporate plans can help to identify whether there will be staff shortages or surpluses in the future. For example, if a new product is planned or future output is going to increase, it may be necessary to take on more staff. Increased mechanisation or a merger with another organisation could result in staff reduction.

Analysis of **past trends** can help a manager to recognise the factors influencing the demand for labour. For example, examination of **seasonal variations** helps to pinpoint times of the year when more staff are required. Fuel merchants are busier in winter, florists are busiest on Valentine's Day and many retailers need extra staff at Christmas.

Mathematical **modelling techniques** using computers and spreadsheets are available to planners to facilitate the preparation of demand forecasts.

Supply of labour

Supply of labour is calculated by examining:
- staff turnover
- the labour market

Besides measuring the future demand for labour, the organisation needs to estimate the availability of workers in the future. This task requires the analysis of **staff turnover** within the organisation and the condition of the **labour market**.

Staff turnover needs to be measured and analysed in order to forecast future losses and also to identify why staff members leave the organisation.

A survey by the Small Firms Association found that in 2007, 17 per cent of the Irish workforce moved jobs. Exit questionnaires show that the main reasons people left their jobs were:
- unhappy with people at work (30 per cent)
- felt contribution was not recognised (25 per cent)
- lack of advancement (20 per cent)
- salary (14 per cent)
- bored with job (5 per cent)

Other reasons why people leave their jobs include:
- job does not live up to expectations
- better pay and conditions elsewhere
- lack of flexible work arrangements
- retirement
- dismissal
- redundancy

Understanding why people leave their jobs can help to increase **staff retention**. For example, if workers tend to leave because the job was not what they expected, methods of recruitment and induction training will have to be examined. If it is because better pay and conditions are being offered somewhere else, then reward strategies may need to be reformed. Retirement is easy to predict by examining the employee age profile. It is also important to identify whether staff retention is a problem in all sections of the organisation or concentrated in just one or a few areas. Reasons for staff turnover can be examined by job attitude questionnaires and exit questionnaires. There are also a number of measurement tools available to managers, such as the turnover index and length of service analysis. See chapter seven for a discussion of employee motivation.

The availability of workers in the **labour market** is another important factor. The organisation needs to be aware of local and national employment levels and of the skill levels of those available for work. It would be unwise to plan for organisational expansion in an area that will not be able to supply the required employees. The existence of competing organisations in the locality will also affect the availability of employees. All of this information needs to be incorporated into the organisation's strategic plans.

> Think of an organisation you are familiar with. What indicators could be used to predict the demand for and supply of workers?

Action planning

Having assessed the organisation's current resources and prepared a forecast of its staffing requirements, it is time to make plans for the future. Beardwell and Claydon (2007, p.175) suggest formulating plans under the following headings:

- **resourcing** – to make better use of existing employees and, where there is a shortage of workers, to recruit new ones (see chapter three)
- **flexibility** – to allow the organisation to respond quickly to its needs in terms of numbers of employees (e.g. relief panels), patterns of hours worked (e.g. annual hours contracts, flexible working hours) and capacity to undertake a variety of tasks (e.g. multiskilling)
- **retention** – to ensure that valued employees stay with the organisation (e.g. improving induction, rewards, communication, work-life balance)
- **downsizing** – to deal with surplus staff (e.g. reduced working hours, redeployment, career breaks, early retirement, voluntary and compulsory redundancy)

Implementation and review

Once plans have been formulated it is imperative that they are **implemented**. The planning process should include an assessment of the resources and methods necessary to put plans into effect, as well as a timetable showing deadlines for implementation of different stages of the strategy. Otherwise, there is a danger that the human resource plans will not be put to use.

It was pointed out at the beginning of this chapter that planning is a continuous process. Once HR plans are made, it does not mean that the organisation has to stick rigidly to them. HR plans are made based on information available at a particular time and it is possible that some of the indicators used to predict the future situation will change. For this reason, the organisation's internal and external environments need to be monitored for any signs of change and plans need to be **reviewed** in light of any changes that occur in these environments.

Finally, the whole human resource planning process needs to be **evaluated** to ensure its effectiveness.

Summary

In this chapter we looked at the human resource planning process. This process is illustrated in figure 2.4.

Important Terms and Concepts

career breaks
competency framework
corporate strategy
demand for labour
downsizing
employee database
employment legislation
evaluate
forecasting
implement and review
job analysis
job description
job sharing

labour market
past trends
person specification
redeployment
reduced working hours
redundancy
retirement
seasonal variations
staff retention
staff turnover
strategic objectives
supply of labour

Revision Questions

1 Why is human resource planning so important?
2 How is HR planning linked to other HR activities?
3 What information should be included in an employee profile?
4 Outline the contents of a job analysis. How is this information compiled?
5 Write a job description, person specification and list of terms and conditions for a job that you are familiar with.
6 Describe some of the indicators used to forecast human resource requirements.
7 Outline the process of human resource planning.

Figure 2.4 *Summary of HR planning process*

Analyse existing situation

Internal environment
- employee profile
- job analysis

External environment
- labour market
- product market
- employment legislation

⇩

Forecast future demand and supply

Demand for labour estimated after considering:
- managerial judgement
- business plans
- past trends
- modelling techniques

Supply of labour is calculated by examining:
- staff turnover
- the labour market

⇩

Formulate plans

- resourcing
- flexibility
- retention
- downsizing

⇩

Implement and review

⇧

3
RECRUITMENT:
ATTRACTING CANDIDATES TO THE ORGANISATION

Objectives

This chapter will help you to:
- distinguish between recruitment and selection
- explain the link between HR planning and the recruitment process
- understand the importance of the job analysis in recruitment
- evaluate different methods of recruitment
- design a recruitment advertisement
- explain the alternatives to recruitment
- describe the possible difficulties in the recruitment process

Definitions

Recruitment and selection are major parts of the employment process. **Recruitment** refers to ways of attracting candidates to the organisation. Methods of attracting potential candidates and encouraging them to apply for vacancies within the organisation will be discussed in this chapter. **Selection** is the part of the process where the successful candidates are chosen from those who applied. Methods of selection will be evaluated in the next chapter.

The Recruitment Process

The recruitment process is linked to the overall HR plan, which in turn stems from the organisation's corporate strategy. Therefore, it is important that line managers as well as HR staff are involved in decision-making at all stages of the recruitment process. The process of recruitment presents a number of challenges to those involved. It is important to keep within the law with regard to **employment equality** (see chapter eleven), and this is particularly relevant today due to the increasing **diversity** within the workforce in terms of age, sex, race, qualifications, backgrounds and so on.

A job vacancy may arise when an employee leaves the organisation, when new positions are created due to expansion or when an employee requests job-sharing arrangements. The first question that arises is whether it is really necessary to replace an employee who has left or whether expansion actually requires the employment of new staff. At this point in the process alternatives to recruitment should be considered and some possible alternatives will be discussed later in the chapter. In more flexible organisations vacancies can arise to allow for job-sharing arrangements.

> Before you read the next section, look back at the section on the job analysis in chapter two. How is this information helpful for the recruitment process?

The job analysis

When there is a vacancy to be filled, a comprehensive examination of the role needs to be carried out. It is important that the recruiter knows as much as possible about the job itself and also what is expected of the individual that fills the vacancy. This information is provided by the job analysis which was described in chapter two. Organisations that engage in human resource planning will have updated job descriptions and person specifications available. These documents provide the starting point for the recruitment process.

The job description and flexibility

When a job description specifies the responsibilities attached to a particular job, the employee may refuse to do any work that is not clearly spelled out. Armstrong (1999, p.300) suggests a way to overcome this potential inflexibility in job descriptions. He recommends that **flexibility** should be built into the job description by 'concentrating on results rather than spelling out what has to be done'. By emphasising the outcome of the job rather than detailing the tasks that lead to that outcome, it is possible to increase the flexibility of the job description and ensure that employees cannot refuse to do work on the basis that it is not in their job description.

> Look back at figure 2.2. Would you say that this job description is flexible? Why (not)?

The information gathered during the job analysis is useful for clarifying precisely what the job entails. It helps the employer to focus on exactly what needs to be done and what kind of person would be best suited to doing it. This information can also facilitate the design of the job advertisement and help to shape the expectations of potential applicants.

Sources of Recruitment

There are a number of ways in which employees can be found to fill a job vacancy. It is important that the organisation invests enough time, resources and analysis in the recruitment process in order to avoid the potential negative outcomes of bad recruiting. If the individual selected for the job turns out to have been a poor choice, the organisation will have to face the cost of a further search. Using inappropriate sources may mean that time and money will be wasted.

The source the organisation chooses depends on the type of job and the availability of workers. Armstrong (1993) suggests that the criteria of cost, speed and the likelihood of providing good candidates should be considered when choosing a recruitment source.

One or more of the following sources can be utilised:
1 Internal search
2 Previous applicants
3 Recommendations
4 Advertising
5 Recruitment agencies
6 Search consultants
7 Colleges and universities
8 Recruitment fairs
9 E-recruitment

> As you read this section, concentrate on how each of these sources can be utilised to attract people to the organisation. What are their strengths and weaknesses?

1 Internal search

It may be possible that the job can be filled by someone already working in the organisation. Internal advertising may help to attract suitable applicants. Much information on the applicant is already available to the organisation through personnel records, including performance appraisals, and from supervisors and colleagues.

One of the strengths of this approach is that information regarding the candidate exists. Moreover, because the employee is familiar with the organisation, it is more likely that their expectations of the job will be met. This reduces the chances of a person leaving in the early stages of employment in a new job. Carl Rogers (1947) is among those writers who believe that people have a natural desire to reach their fullest potential. A policy of filling vacancies from within can therefore serve to motivate workers. Indeed, in some organisations, internal recruitment may be one of the outcomes of negotiations with unions. Finally, this method of recruitment is fast and inexpensive.

However, searching within the organisation for someone to fill a vacancy limits the pool of potential applicants, as qualified and experienced individuals outside the company are automatically excluded from the process. Furthermore, it may be more beneficial for the organisation to look outside for someone with new ideas and new ways of doing things. There is also the danger that staff who have not been selected may become demotivated. Another drawback of the internal search is that having found someone within the organisation to fill the vacancy, another vacancy now exists.

2 *Previous applicants*

Even if the attempt to fill the vacancy internally is not successful, there are other fast and inexpensive ways of finding potential employees. Looking through the CVs and application forms that people have sent in recently may identify a suitable candidate. These CVs and application forms may have been received by the organisation as job applications or simply by people enquiring about current openings. An individual who was unsuccessful in a previous application to the organisation could be the right person for the job in this instance.

3 *Recommendations*

Asking current employees if they know anyone suitable could be effective. Such recommendations can be useful because the employee should be able to give a realistic description of the job and the company to the potential candidate.

While using employee recommendations to find new employees is probably most common in low-skilled jobs, this method is not confined to such work. In times of high employment, companies may turn to their high-skilled, professional employees in the hope that they have similarly qualified friends in other organisations. Indeed some companies offer financial incentives to their employees for making successful recommendations.

However, as with the internal search, the pool of potential candidates is narrowed if previous applications and employee recommendations are relied upon.

It may be worth contacting people who have worked for the organisation in the past to see if they are interested in returning. These individuals are familiar with the organisation and how it operates. Moreover, the suitability of these people can easily be confirmed by speaking to colleagues and supervisors, as well as by checking performance appraisal records.

4 Advertising

The organisation may decide not to confine its search for new workers to the existing workforce and their contacts. The decision to extend the search may be made in an effort to widen the pool of potential applicants. In some cases, particularly in the public sector, there may be a legal obligation to advertise certain positions externally. This is to ensure open competition and avoid the possibility of nepotism.

Advertising the job vacancy in national **newspapers** or **specialist magazines** can be expensive, but the message reaches a larger number of potential applicants. In Ireland, *The Irish Times* on Fridays and Thursday's *Irish Independent* have supplements devoted to job vacancies. While these sources are commonly used to recruit professional and managerial staff, it is equally usual to find small ads in local newspapers advertising lower skilled jobs. Jobs can also be advertised on radio **jobspots**, **teletext** and the **Internet**.

Choice of location for an advertisement depends on the type of job, advertising budget, target audience and time available. Job advertisements have the additional benefit of increasing the organisation's public profile.

Designing the advertisement

In order to avoid unwanted applications, the advertisement should be designed in such a way as to attract suitable candidates, while deterring unsuitable candidates from applying. It may be of benefit to engage the services of a specialist advertising agency for advice and guidance on how to produce high impact recruitment advertising. In any case, the following information should be included in the advertisement:
- company name and information about the company
- job title and responsibilities
- the person required
- pay and benefits
- statement of policy on issues such as equal opportunities
- how to apply
- closing date for applications

5 Recruitment agencies

As the search for new employees can be time-consuming and requires a certain amount of skill, the organisation may choose to engage the services of a recruitment agency. Collins McNicholas, Grafton Recruitment and ICE are examples of large recruitment agencies in Ireland. Such agencies are often used to find clerical and secretarial staff as well as managerial personnel. In addition, many agencies specialise in finding staff in particular industries, such as engineering, catering or IT.

It is important to ensure that the agency is clear about the organisation's staffing requirements in order to avoid the selection of unsuitable candidates. This is an expensive way of finding staff as the agency charges a fee based on a percentage of a year's salary. A major advantage is that the recruitment process is left to professionals and this saves time and work for the organisation.

FÁS provides a free service to employers who wish to recruit new staff.

6 Search consultants

Search consultants, or **'head-hunters'**, are often used to fill senior management positions. Search consultants have a network of contacts and can identify suitable people in other organisations. Potential candidates are approached directly and informally by the head-hunter to discuss the possibility of taking up a job elsewhere. This is probably the most expensive source of recruitment, with search consultants charging a fee of 30 to 50 per cent of the first year's salary. MERC Partners is a well-known search consultancy in Ireland.

7 Colleges and universities

Some organisations try to identify potential employees before they graduate. Typically, representatives visit colleges once a year and present information on their organisation to final year students and advise them of job opportunities that exist. Some organisations offer graduate trainee programmes for recent graduates.

One of the main advantages to the organisation of recruiting straight from college is that these new employees should be up to date on the latest developments in their area of study. However, they may not have much work experience.

8 Recruitment fairs

Employers can attend recruitment fairs as part of the recruitment process. At recruitment fairs, employers are invited, for a fee, to set up a stand and provide information about job opportunities in their organisations.

Recruitment fairs put employers in contact with people who are either currently unemployed or thinking of changing jobs. Organisations which exhibit at recruitment fairs also have the opportunity to increase their public profile. The cost to the employer varies. Attending a jobs fair in a college will be relatively inexpensive but exhibiting at a major recruitment fair abroad can be quite costly.

9 E-recruitment

E-recruitment is a general term that refers to the use of information technology in the recruitment process. Organisations can advertise vacancies on their website or through the websites of recruitment agencies such as www.irishjobs.ie, www.myjob.ie and www.recruitireland.com. According to the 2010 CIPD survey, *Resourcing and Talent Planning*, the most effective method for attracting candidates is the organisation's own website. This is particularly the case for the voluntary, community, not-for-profit and public services sectors. The survey also reported that professional networking sites, such as LinkedIn, were rated as the most effective by almost 20 per cent of respondents from the private services sector.

One of the main advantages of using the Internet as a source of recruitment is that a lot of information about the job and the organisation can be supplied to prospective applicants. E-recruitment can also be a cheaper and faster way of filling vacancies and has the potential to reach a wider pool of applicants. Furthermore, use of modern technology portrays an image of an up-to-date organisation and so can strengthen an employer's brand.

A key concern regarding e-recruitment is the danger of excluding applicants who are not comfortable using technology. Another drawback is that it may increase the number of unsuitable applicants, thus creating more work for those who are responsible for shortlisting candidates for interview.

An overview of the sources of recruitment can be found in the summary section of this chapter.

Think of an organisation you are familiar with. Identify the sources of recruitment which are most suitable for finding employees and explain your choice.

Alternatives to Recruitment

When a job vacancy arises in an organisation it may not be necessary to recruit a new employee. HR and line managers should first consider whether a job really exists, and whether the tasks involved in the job still need to be carried out. Taking on a new employee is only one possible solution.

> Can you think of ways to ensure that the job is carried out without recruiting new staff?

Here are some alternatives to recruitment:
1 Subcontracting
2 Automation
3 Overtime
4 Job enlargement or job enrichment

1 Subcontracting

In some organisations, cleaning, catering and security staff are not direct employees of the organisation. They are employed by subcontractors who organise rosters, pay wages and solve staffing problems such as absenteeism. Subcontracting is common in the building industry and in computer programming, where people are subcontracted to work on specific projects. By using subcontractors, the organisation can avoid the many employer responsibilities involved in finding and training staff, but it results in reduced organisational control over the subcontracted employees.

2 Automation

There are situations where new technology or equipment may replace employees. For example, the banking industry has responded to consumer demand for more flexible and convenient banking hours by installing ATMs and adopting Internet banking instead of lengthening bank opening hours and employing more staff. Automation is common in industries that previously required a lot of skill, such as printing and textile production. However, this alternative to recruitment usually requires heavy financial investment.

3 Overtime

If the organisation only requires extra staff in the short term, it may be useful to offer overtime work to existing employees, who might welcome the opportunity to earn extra money. Since recruitment and selection can be an expensive and time-consuming process, it might not be worth employing someone new for a short period of time. However, there is a danger when offering overtime that the regular work is deliberately prolonged to create more overtime hours. The Organisation of Working Time Act (1997) limits the average working week to forty-eight hours. Averaging may be balanced out over a four-month period, or for six or twelve months in certain circumstances.

4 Job enlargement or job enrichment

Another way to manage the vacancy is to divide the workload among existing staff. Job enlargement involves combining smaller tasks into one job. Job enrichment entails giving workers more tasks to perform and more control and responsibility over how they are performed. New job descriptions may have to be written to incorporate any extra tasks and responsibilities assigned to employees.

Constraints on Recruitment

This section outlines some of the obstacles the organisation may encounter when attempting to employ new workers.

> Think of an organisation you know. Are there any reasons why it might have difficulty in attracting new employees? What are they?

Constraints on recruitment include:
1 Reputation of organisation or profession
2 Nature of the job
3 Costs
4 Employment legislation
5 Lack of necessary specialist skills

1 Reputation of organisation or profession

The organisation may encounter some obstacles when attempting to employ new workers. Recruiting new employees can be difficult if either the organisation or the profession has a bad image or reputation. Work practices or industrial relations problems may negatively influence the perception of potential applicants.

2 Nature of the job

Some vacancies are difficult to fill due to the nature of the job itself. It may be perceived to be unpleasant, dangerous, badly paid or too stressful. The hospitality industry finds it difficult to recruit and retain staff because of the unsociable working hours and poor pay.

3 Costs

The process of recruiting and selecting staff can be quite expensive depending on the methods used. In addition, the employer has a number of financial obligations to the new worker which may prove to be prohibitive. Apart from salary or wages, the employer is obliged to make PRSI contributions for each member of staff.

4 Employment legislation

The Employment Equality Acts (1998–2008) oblige an employer to provide equal employment opportunities to potential candidates. This is particularly relevant today, due to the increasing diversity within the workforce in terms of age, sex, race, qualifications and backgrounds. For more information on this legislation, see chapter eleven.

5 Lack of necessary specialist skills

In some cases it can take a long time to fill a vacancy because it is hard to find the set of skills required by the organisation, particularly in management positions. The 2010 CIPD survey, *Resourcing and Talent Planning*, reports that 67 per cent of organisations gave this as the main reason for recruitment difficulties.

Summary

Vacancy arises because:
- employee leaves
- organisation expands
- employee requests job-sharing arrangements

Examine the documents produced during the job analysis:
- job description
- person specification
- terms and conditions

Choose method(s) of recruitment:

Table 3.1 *Summary of recruitment sources*

Method	Advantages	Disadvantages
Internal search	• applicant knows organisation and vice versa • fast • inexpensive • can help motivation	• narrows pool of applicants • organisation may need new blood • still have a vacancy to fill • may have negative effect on motivation
Previous applicants	• information on candidates already available • quick • inexpensive	• narrows pool of applicants • may no longer be available
Recommendations	• contacts made through existing employees • applicants may be familiar with organisational culture	• narrows pool of candidates • may be too similar to existing employees
Advertising	• open competition • increases profile of organisation • large number of potential candidates	• can be expensive
Recruitment agencies	• professional recruiters • saves time for organisation	• very expensive

Method	Advantages	Disadvantages
Search consultants	• have useful contacts • can identify suitable people	• very expensive
Colleges and universities	• up-to-date qualifications • can be trained in way to suit organisation	• little or no work experience
Recruitment fairs	• attract interested people • increase organisation's profile	• may be expensive
E-recruitment	• fast • inexpensive • good for organisation's image	• excludes candidates who are uncomfortable using technology

Consider the alternatives to recruitment:
- subcontracting
- automation
- overtime
- job enlargement or job enrichment

Keep in mind the constraints on recruiting:
- reputation of organisation or profession
- the job itself
- cost
- legislation
- lack of necessary specialist skills

Important Terms and Concepts

advertising	e-recruitment
automation	head-hunter
colleges and universities	inflexibility
constraints on recruitment	internal search
corporate strategy	Internet
diversity	job analysis
employment equality legislation	job enlargement

job enrichment	recruitment agencies
overtime	recruitment fair
previous applicants	search consultants
recommendation	selection
recruitment	subcontracting

Revision Questions

1 Explain the difference between recruitment and selection.
2 Why are job descriptions sometimes inflexible? How can this inflexibility be reduced?
3 Evaluate the sources of recruitment available to the human resource manager.
4 What should be included in a job advertisement?
5 Describe the constraints on the recruiting process that might affect the organisation.
6 Discuss the alternatives to recruitment.

4
SELECTION:
CHOOSING THE RIGHT PERSON FOR THE JOB

Objectives

This chapter will help you to:
- define human resource selection
- explain why the interview is such a popular method of selection
- outline the reasons why the interview is not the best predictor of future work performance
- discuss ways to improve the interviewing process
- describe the different types of psychological tests
- evaluate a number of methods of employee selection

Definition

Heery and Noon (2001, p.320) define human resource selection as 'the process of assessing job applicants using one or a variety of methods with the purpose of finding the most suitable person for the organisation'.

The Selection Process

If the recruitment campaign (see chapter three) has been successful, there should be a number of job applications to be considered. The next stage in the employment process involves choosing the best person from those who have applied. You will remember that in chapter one **integration** was discussed as a distinguishing characteristic of human resource management. The selection process provides an opportunity for integration, as both HR managers and line managers have an important role to play in choosing who will be employed by the organisation. Moreover, the selection process involves integration with other HR activities such as planning and training. Throughout the process of selection, care must be taken not to discriminate against any candidate on the basis of age, race, gender and so on, as applicants are protected by the Employment Equality Acts (1998–2008) (see chapter eleven).

Objectives of the selection process

Foot and Hook (2008) outline the main objectives of the selection process as follows:
- gather as much relevant information as possible about the candidates
- organise and evaluate the information
- assess each candidate in order to forecast performance on the job
- give information to candidates so that they can judge whether or not they wish to accept an offer of employment

Methods of Selection

There are many criteria for choosing the right person for a job. A manager in a large multi-national company based in Ireland recounted a situation where a candidate was taken out to lunch by his prospective employers. It was quickly decided that he would not be offered the job because he had put salt on his food before tasting it!

There are a number of more conventional methods available for selecting a person to fill a job vacancy. The interview tends to be the central selection method but is often supplemented by one or more of the other selection techniques.

The following methods will be evaluated in this chapter:
1　Shortlisting
2　The selection interview
3　Psychological testing
4　Work samples
5　Situational exercises
6　Biographical data (biodata)
7　Assessment centres
8　References
9　E-selection

1 Shortlisting

Shortlisting is a stage between recruitment and selection and is necessary in situations where a large number of applications are received. Shortlisting involves reducing the applications to a more manageable number by narrowing down the field of applicants who will continue to the next stage of the selection process. Two methods of shortlisting are outlined below:

Method 1   Compare the person specification or competency framework (see chapter two) against the application form or curriculum vitae of each candidate to decide whether they meet the requirements of the job. Candidates who do not possess the criteria deemed as 'essential' can be eliminated.

Method 2   Look at the person specification or competency framework and give points for each criterion that the candidate meets. Add up the points and eliminate the lowest ranking candidates.

> Before you read the next section, write down as many reasons as you can think of for why the interview is such a popular method of selection. Check your answers as you read on.

2 The selection interview

Reasons for its popularity

An interview, however informal, is part of almost every selection process. There are many reasons for its popularity. It provides the opportunity for the manager to meet the potential employee **face to face**. Most of us have a tendency to trust our own **intuition** and believe that we are good judges of character so the prospect of employing someone without ever meeting them seems foolish. The interview provides an opportunity for the interviewer to **obtain information** about the candidates, **communicate information** about the job and **clarify** applicants' questions. It can be carried out almost **anywhere** and **no special equipment** is required. The interview is usually **faster** and **cheaper** than methods such as psychological testing or assessment centres. The costs involved in interviewing can vary widely depending on the procedures followed. The process becomes expensive if, for example, a large number of applicants are interviewed and have their travel expenses paid. The interview is suitable for selecting people into **all types of jobs**.

Reasons why the interview can be a poor predictor of future performance

Although it is the most popular way to choose people for jobs, evidence (e.g. Reilly and Chao, 1982) suggests that the unstructured interview is not always the best method of predicting future performance at work. Quite often, interviewers have had little training in interviewing techniques and may underestimate some of the limitations of perception and memory. Some possible reasons why the interview is such a poor predictor of future performance are:

- lack of interviewer preparation
- interview has no structure
- questions do not relate to the job
- problems remembering candidates' responses
- perceptual limitations of the interviewer
- interviewer talks too much

> Now that you are aware of some of the problems with the interview process, suggest ways to improve it. You should think about this question from the point of view of the interviewer.

Steps to improve the interview procedure

i) Prepare for the interview The average interview lasts for approximately thirty to forty minutes. This does not give the interviewer much time to get to know the candidate or to decide whether the individual is suitable for the job or not. This is why the interviewer needs to prepare beforehand in order to make best use of the interview time. It is important that time is spent before the interview reading the application form and matching the candidate's details against the person specification. **Preparation** of this kind is essential, as it gives the interviewer the opportunity to identify key aspects of the application that can be focused on during the course of the interview. An interviewer who is inadequately prepared may miss some important pieces of information and make a decision based on insufficient or irrelevant information.

ii) Design the structure of the interview The interview should have an opening, a middle and a closing. The objectives of the opening stage are to make introductions, establish rapport and explain the purpose of the interview. The main aims of the middle part are to ask relevant questions and provide information to the candidate. The closing stage allows the candidate to clarify any outstanding issues and make final comments. The interviewer should inform the candidate of what happens next in the selection process.

Within this structure, decisions need to be made about what questions the candidate should be asked. If each candidate is asked different questions, this makes comparison of candidates' responses difficult. While following the planned structure facilitates comparison later, it is important to allow for a certain amount of flexibility too. Sticking rigidly to the list of questions may mean that certain interesting points made during the interview are not followed up.

iii) Ask relevant questions The traditional **biographical interview** goes through the education and work experience of the candidate with the aim of building up a picture of what the person is like. For example, a candidate might be asked why they chose a certain career or course of study. The problem with this style of interviewing is that the information obtained during the interview is not enough on its own to predict the individual's future performance at work.

The **situational-based interview** describes typical situations or problems that the candidate may experience in the job and asks the candidate what they would do. For example, a sales assistant could be asked how they would deal with an angry customer making a complaint. While this style of interviewing obtains an indication of how the candidate might deal with certain situations in theory, it is not certain how situations would be handled in practice.

Competency-based interviews assume that evidence of past performance and behaviour is the best predictor of future performance and behaviour. Candidates are asked to describe how they dealt with particular situations in the past. The questions asked in this type of interview are chosen very carefully (with the help of the competency framework or person specification discussed in chapter two) to ensure that they relate to the competencies relevant for the job. If a job requires good decision-making skills, the candidate could be asked to give a specific example of how they arrived at a particular work-related decision. The main drawback of this approach is that the preparation is time-consuming and interviewers need training in the technique.

Lack of **job relatedness** in the questions may lead to the selection of an unsuitable employee. Whatever style or mixture of styles is chosen, it is important that the questions asked are relevant to the job.

iv) Take notes Even after a short interview it can be difficult to remember the answers that a candidate gave to each question asked. When a number of candidates have been interviewed it is even more difficult to remember what each person said at the end of the day. This is why it is important to make notes of each candidate's responses during the interview. At a panel interview, when one member of the panel is asking questions, another can record the answers given. These interview notes should be kept for at least one year. They will be required if an unsuccessful candidate requests feedback from the interview or takes a case against the employer.

v) Be aware of perceptual limitations Most people need to make sense of other people and situations and what is going on around them. We also have a tendency to satisfy this need with very little information. The perceptual errors discussed below have one thing in common: they all reflect efforts to evaluate people and situations based on either inadequate or irrelevant information. The interviewer must realise that perceptual abilities are limited and that because of this we have a tendency to make errors when evaluating other people. Trained interviewers are aware of these tendencies and can try to reduce their effects.

Stereotyping occurs when we try to categorise people according to characteristics such as age, sex, address, education, school attended, accent, race and so on. The problem is that we sometimes jump to conclusions about people based on this kind of information. We cannot assume that all old people are resistant to change or that all people living in a certain area are wealthy. It is particularly important that interviewers become aware of their biases as there is legislation in place to ensure equal opportunities and to protect people from discrimination. (See *Gleeson v Rotunda and Mater Hospitals, Hughes v Aer Lingus, Freeman v Superquinn and O'Neill v Board of Management, St Gabriel's National School* in chapter eleven.)

The **halo effect** is a tendency to focus on one positive characteristic of the candidate and to generalise and assume the candidate has other positive characteristics. For example, the interviewer might notice that the interviewee has achieved very high academic standards and assume that they will reach high standards of performance in the workplace too. The **horns effect** is the tendency to generalise from one negative characteristic.

People have a tendency to focus more at the beginning of things and to remember the start better. This is called the **primacy effect**. Since people feel they need to understand situations, even if they only have sketchy information to help them reach their conclusions, they tend to make judgements quite quickly based on early information. If this happens at an interview, added to the fact that we trust our own intuition, the interviewer is likely to make a decision on a candidate right at the start and try to justify this initial decision for the duration of the interview.

There is a danger too that the interviewer's judgement of a candidate will be influenced by the performance of the previous candidate. This is called the **contrast effect** and implies that if the previous candidate is excellent, the next will not be seen to be as good as they really are. Similarly, if the first candidate performs badly, the next candidate can appear better than they really are.

vi) Don't dominate the interview Untrained and inexperienced interviewers sometimes do most of the talking during the interview. It is recommended that the interviewee speaks for at least 80 per cent of the interview time. The corollary of this is that the interviewer should be **listening** for 80 per cent of the time. The interviewer needs to be able to concentrate on what the candidate is saying in order to take in as much information as possible. A good interviewer can formulate questions that encourage the candidate to speak freely. **Open questions** begin with words like what, why or how, and cannot be answered with just 'yes' or 'no'.

vii) Use a panel Using a panel to select an employee is fairer than the one-to-one approach, as selection is based on the opinions of more than one interviewer. This reduces the effects of interviewer bias and subjectivity. Panel members may have different areas of expertise, all relevant to the position. It could be that a number of people have a vested interest in the new post holder and so their involvement in the selection process is required.

Finding a date and time to suit all panel members may be difficult. While using a panel could lead to better decision-making, there is always the danger that a dominant panel member could influence other panel members in their evaluations of candidates.

Make sure you understand what you have just read.

Write down the main points under the heading 'Ways to improve the interviewing process'.

The next section outlines some of the other methods used to select new employees. As you read, concentrate on their usefulness as part of the selection process.

---

3 Psychological testing

Psychological tests (also known as psychometric tests) assess characteristics which are related to satisfactory job performance. They add objectivity and fairness to the selection process and measure some factors that cannot be assessed through the application form and the interview. All candidates do the same tests under the same conditions and responses are scored impartially. Many of the psychological tests used in the selection process have been researched extensively and special training is required to administer them. Psychological testing is applicable in all kinds of job situations and costs vary depending on the particular test.

Types of psychological tests

Intelligence tests are used as a means of selecting people for jobs in the belief that a certain amount of intelligence is needed for job success. The logic follows that these tests can identify those who are not smart enough to do the job. There are a number of intelligence tests available for business uses, such as the Graduate Management Admission Test. One of the criticisms of intelligence tests is that they may be biased in favour of white middle-class people. Another criticism is that it is difficult to predict future performance based on intelligence.

Ability tests measure job-related characteristics such as typing or mechanical ability. Eyesight and hearing tests are other examples of abilities that may be assessed as part of the selection process. **Aptitude tests** are designed to measure the **potential** an individual has to do a particular job. Aptitude and ability tests are most suited for jobs where specific and measurable skills are required. They are useful for shortlisting from a large number of candidates.

Personality tests are used to measure certain personality traits and to predict work behaviour. The Big Five Personality Model assesses levels of extroversion/introversion, emotional stability, agreeableness, conscientiousness and openness (Roberts, 1997). Personality tests may be appropriate when the job involves a lot of interpersonal contact or when certain personality characteristics are important for the job. However, those who criticise the use of personality tests in selection doubt the stability of personality over time and question the predictive value of these tests.

More organisations are using psychological testing as part of the selection procedure. Use of psychological tests should be restricted to reputable ones and administered only by properly trained staff.

4 Work samples

Work samples are designed to be a sample of the candidate's behaviour and performance on the job. The employer can observe the candidate's level of competency on a particular task and the candidate has the opportunity to experience the kind of work they will be doing if their application is successful. Obvious examples include a typing test and a driving test, but work samples could also involve asking the candidate to assemble a component or use a piece of equipment.

Work samples are job relevant and are more appropriate for selecting people with a trade, such as a plumber, carpenter or electrician, where there is one best way to complete a task. They are less well suited to jobs that involve working with people, such as social workers, where there may be a number of ways of dealing with a situation. This method can be quite expensive and creating a work sample can be time-consuming. Work samples are usually administered individually, which requires more time.

5 Situational exercises

These are sometimes referred to as white collar work samples. Situational exercises are used most frequently to select people for administrative and managerial jobs. An example of a situational exercise is the **In-tray exercise**. Candidates are given samples of work that they could expect to find in the 'in-tray' on their desks and asked to deal with them. This could include writing memos, making phone calls, preparing reports and letters, prioritising and decision-making. **Role-plays** are another example of situational exercises and are particularly relevant for jobs which involve working with people, such as customer services or counselling. Situational exercises are job relevant and can give a good indication of a candidate's likely performance on the job. This method of selection is quite time-consuming.

6 Biographical data (biodata)

The use of biographical data is one of the oldest and simplest ways to select a person for a job. Using biodata to select employees is based on the belief that past activities and behaviours help predict future activities and behaviours. This method usually requires a questionnaire to be completed, but much of the information is available from application forms and CVs. This method is applicable across all types of jobs and is inexpensive. Although some research seems to indicate that biodata is one of the best methods of selection (e.g. Muchinsky, 1986) there is a difficulty in linking biographical information to future job performance. In addition, there is a danger that items of biographical information, such as age and marital status, could be used to discriminate against applicants.

7 Assessment centres

An assessment centre refers to a *process* of selection, not a place. It is mostly used for selection into managerial or supervisory positions. The assessment process usually lasts for one or two days. The candidates are assessed in a number of ways and by a number of assessors. Methods used include interviews, psychological tests, work samples and situational exercises, group discussions, self-assessment and peer assessment. The exercises used in the assessment centre must be designed to assess relevant job competencies which have been clearly identified by managers and job holders. One of the advantages of assessment centres is that several candidates can be assessed at the same time. Moreover, the fact that a number of selection techniques are used in combination improves the quality of decision-making. However, this is probably the most expensive selection method of all.

8 References

Checking candidates' references is the final step in the selection process. The new employer contacts the candidate's previous employer to:
- confirm the details on the CV or application form
- get new information
- predict future performance

Using references as part of the selection procedure is inexpensive but it is difficult to know how fair it is. In many cases candidates choose their referees and it is unlikely that they would ask someone who will give them a bad reference. Employers need to be careful when wording references. The Freedom of Information Act (1997) might make the process more transparent, but referees may be hesitant to disclose negative information for fear of legal action.

9 E-selection

Technology can be used to aid the selection process. For example, questionnaires can be built into the online application process and used to compile a shortlist of candidates. Online testing can also form part of the selection process. A 2009 CIPD survey, *Recruitment, Retention and Turnover*, indicated that 17 per cent of respondents use online selection tests.

> Go online and look at the vacancies section of an organisation you would like to work for. Assess how this organisation uses technology for recruitment and selection.

Evaluating Methods of Selection

When deciding which method(s) of selection to employ, the following criteria need to be considered:
- **validity** – does the method measure what it is supposed to measure? In other words, does an intelligence test really test intelligence?
- **reliability** – does the method produce the same result every time? Does the method produce the same result if carried out by different people?
- **fairness** – is this method unbiased toward different subgroups of applicants e.g. race, sex?
- **applicability** – can this method be used for many job types?
- **cost** – is it expensive?
- **acceptability** – is this method acceptable to both the candidate and the employer?

To get a clearer understanding of the strengths and weaknesses of the methods of selection discussed above, complete table 4.1. Most of these answers can be found in the text and for those that have not been mentioned specifically, think about them yourself. When you have finished, check your answers with those in table 4.2 in the summary section of this chapter. This table is based on the work of Muchinsky (1986).

Table 4.1 *Evaluation of selection methods*

Method	Validity	Reliability	Fairness	Applicability	Cost	Acceptability
Interview						
Intelligence tests						
Aptitude and ability tests						
Personality tests						
Work samples						
Situational exercises						
Biographical data						
Assessment centres						
References						

Summary

The chapter began with an outline of the objectives of the selection process.

This was followed by a discussion of a number of selection methods, in particular the interview.

Suggestions were made on how to improve the interview as a selection tool.

Finally, criteria for evaluating the methods of selection were explained. These criteria are applied in table 4.2 below.

Table 4.2 *Evaluation of selection methods*

Method	Validity	Reliability	Fairness	Applicability	Cost	Acceptability
Interview	*can be low depends on standard of interview*	*low*	*moderate*	*high*	*moderate —low*	*high*
Intelligence tests	*moderate*	*high*	*moderate*	*high*	*low*	*moderate*
Aptitude and ability tests	*moderate*	*high*	*high*	*moderate*	*low*	*high*
Personality tests	*moderate*	*moderate*	*high*	*low*	*moderate*	*moderate*
Work samples	*high*	*high*	*high*	*low*	*high*	*high*
Situational exercises	*moderate*	*unknown*	*unknown*	*low*	*moderate*	*high*
Biographical data	*high*	*unknown*	*moderate*	*high*	*low*	*high*
Assessment centres	*high*	*unknown*	*high*	*low*	*high*	*moderate*
References	*low*	*questionable*	*unknown*	*high*	*low*	*high*

Important Terms and Concepts

ability tests
aptitude tests
assessment centres
biographical data
biographical interview
competency-based interview
contrast effect
e-selection
halo effect
horns effect
intelligence tests
interview
interview structure
interviewer dominance
in-tray exercise

job relatedness
panel interview
perceptual limitations
personality tests
preparation
primacy effect
psychological testing
references
role-plays
selection process
shortlist
situational exercises
situational-based interview
stereotyping
work samples

Revision Questions

1 Why is the interview such a popular method of selection?
2 Outline some of the reasons why the interview can be a poor predictor of future performance at work.
3 Draw up a list of guidelines for improving the interview process.
4 Describe the different types of psychological testing and comment on their usefulness.
5 Write notes on the following methods of selection:
   - work samples
   - situational exercises
   - biographical data
   - assessment centres
   - references

SECTION 3

MANAGING PERFORMANCE

What can be done to maximise employee performance in order to reach organisational goals?

This HR function requires managers to monitor and improve employee performance by integrating training and development methods, performance evaluation methods, motivation processes and payment systems, in order to achieve organisational objectives.

5
HUMAN RESOURCE DEVELOPMENT

Objectives

This chapter will help you to:
- define human resource development
- distinguish between training, development and learning
- understand the importance of training and development in the organisation
- discuss the factors that influence an organisation's training and development policy
- identify the key elements of the stages in the training process
- examine different techniques used for training and development
- evaluate the training process
- describe induction training

Definitions

According to Armstrong (2006, p.533), '**Human resource development (HRD)** is concerned with the provision of learning, development and training opportunities in order to improve individual, team and organisational performance'.

Gunnigle *et al.* (2006, p.233) define the terms learning, development and training.

Learning is a process through which people assimilate new knowledge and skills that result in relatively permanent changes in behaviour. Learning can be conscious or unconscious, formal or informal, and requires some element of practice and experience.

Development refers to the acquisition of skills and abilities that are required for future roles in the company.

Training refers to the acquisition of the knowledge, skills and abilities required to perform effectively in a given role.

Therefore, human resource development incorporates the achievement of both general and specific knowledge, skills and abilities, for present and future purposes, through a variety of means.

The Importance of HR Development

An organisation's most valuable resource is its employees, who can be the key to competitive advantage. Employers and managers must ensure that employees are equipped to meet the present and future demands necessary for competitive functioning. This requires the strategic linking of training and development activities to corporate objectives and the involvement of line managers in HRD. Some of the reasons for training and development are to:

- produce quality goods in a shorter time
- reduce accidents in the workplace
- introduce new technology
- facilitate change
- improve service
- retain good employees
- increase motivation
- meet employees' needs
- create and sustain an effective management team
- promote **continuing professional development**

In times of economic recession, organisations often cut back on their training budgets. However, a 2009 CIPD guide entitled *Promoting the Value of Learning in Adversity* proposes that HRD is the key to surviving difficult economic times. The guide suggests that organisations which continue to invest in staff development will be in a better position to compete when the economic situation improves.

Training and Development Policy

Organisations' attitudes to training and development differ. The policy of some organisations is to avoid training their employees as it is an unnecessary expense. At the other end of the spectrum exists the **learning organisation**.

In learning organisations training and development is viewed as having an important role in improving organisational performance and is allocated the necessary resources. The 'learning organisation' is a particular strategy that an organisation may choose to adopt, but is not necessarily the best strategy for every organisation given the difficulty and expense associated with its implementation.

Think about organisations that you are familiar with. What is their attitude towards training and what do you think influences this attitude?

An organisation's training policy is influenced by the following considerations.

Management trends Organisations that are shifting their style of management toward HRM are more likely to encourage and support a learning environment. This is because development of the human resource is believed to benefit the organisation.

Employment legislation An organisation may be legally obliged to provide certain training. For example, health and safety is a major issue in the construction industry at the moment. The Safety, Health and Welfare at Work Act (2005) states that the organisation must prepare a safety statement and take steps to deal with any risks or hazards in the workplace. Training needs to be provided to ensure that employees can identify dangers at work and know how to operate dangerous equipment and machinery. See chapter eleven for more details of employment legislation.

The labour market If there are not enough suitably trained people available in the labour market, then the organisation will have no choice but to provide the training itself. There is less pressure on an organisation to provide training when skilled labour is available or can be poached from other organisations.

Available resources Training and development can require time, money, space, equipment and qualified trainers. It is easier to become a learning organisation when these resources are available. Lack of necessary resources forces an organisation to reduce or eliminate plans for training and development.

The Development Process

There are three phases in the development process: preparation, training–development and evaluation.

The preparation phase

It is important that some preparation is done before a particular training or development programme is chosen. This is to help ensure the success of the programme once it is implemented.

> Before you read on, what kind of preparation do you think is necessary?

The organisation needs to:
- identify training needs
- set specific objectives
- ensure organisational support for the programme

- allocate the necessary resources
- facilitate the transfer of learning

A training need is the 'gap' between desired performance and actual performance. The first stage in the process is to carry out a **needs analysis** to assess what kind of training or development is required in the organisation. Training may be needed when the organisation:
- takes on a new employee
- carries out a performance appraisal
- introduces new technology
- responds to changes in legislation
- wants to improve the quantity and quality of work
- establishes new work practices
- decides to provide new products or services

The **specific objectives** to be achieved through the training and development programme should be established at the start, as these will be used to evaluate whether or not the training and development programme has been successful. Examples of objectives set for trainees include being able to operate a cash register, assemble a piece of equipment or close a sale.

The preparation stage also involves getting **organisational support** for the programme. This is necessary because training can interrupt workers' daily routines and the cooperation of managers and workers is an important factor in the success or failure of the programme.

Another aspect of preparation is to ensure that all the **necessary resources** are available. Resources include people who are qualified to carry out the training, the necessary equipment, money and space.

When training is completed, participants must have the opportunity to **transfer new skills** as soon as possible. Equipment used during training should be similar to the equipment used on the job. If possible ease the pressure of work for trainees for a short time after returning to work to give them a chance to practise their new skills.

The training–development phase

This section discusses the following methods of training and development:
- demonstration
- coaching
- mentoring
- job rotation
- internal and external courses

- open or distance learning
- workshops
- e-learning

> As you read, focus on their strengths and weaknesses and think about what kind of jobs they are suitable for.

Demonstration is a commonly used training technique. A supervisor or colleague shows the trainee how to do the job and then lets them do it themselves. This method is sometimes called 'Sitting next to Nellie'. This is an inexpensive method of training for the organisation to use and there is a high transfer of learning as the trainee actively participates in the training process. In addition, the trainee is learning from someone who actually does the job and training takes place within the organisation.

The problem with this method is that there is usually no structure in the procedure and it may turn out to be a time-consuming way of training the employee. Quite often the colleague who demonstrates does not have any training skills and so may not be able to explain well how to do certain things or why they are done. In fact, the individual chosen to demonstrate to the trainee might resent having to do so and see it as an inconvenience which delays their own work. The trainee may pick up their colleague's bad habits such as taking shortcuts and not following procedures correctly. In addition, the feedback from a colleague may not be constructive.

Coaching is a technique usually used for trainees in managerial or supervisory positions. Planned meetings take place between the trainee and their immediate manager where the trainee can be given guidance on how to deal with situations. It often involves a certain amount of delegation of responsibility from the superior to the trainee. Such an approach to training is job relevant as the trainee is being guided in carrying out the duties of the job. However, unless it is properly planned as part of the training process, pressures of time on the part of the superior may limit the amount of individual attention that can be given.

Mentoring bears a number of similarities to coaching. However, whereas the coach tends to be the individual's immediate superior, the mentor is more often a more senior manager and not always in the same area of responsibility. Coaching is one aspect of mentoring. Gibb and Megginson (1993) identified four mentoring roles:
- helping to improve performance
- helping career development
- acting as a counsellor
- sharing knowledge

This method of management development is useful for preparing potential managers for a future role. This is known as **succession planning**. However, establishing a formal mentoring programme may be difficult due to the amount of time and effort involved on the part of the mentor. It may not be easy to find a manager with mentoring skills and the commitment required.

Job rotation is a training technique which involves moving people from job to job or department to department to broaden their experience. It is more often used with management trainees. Job rotation is an inexpensive method of job training and it gives the trainee the opportunity to acquire knowledge and skills in different parts of the organisation. For this type of training to be successful it is important that a programme is designed which specifies what the trainee is expected to learn at each placement. Otherwise this method can lack direction and prove inefficient.

Employees can be sent on **courses** for training and development. These courses can be designed specifically for the needs of the organisation and take place internally, or employees can be sent to classes run by computer training centres, management institutes and so on. Designing **internal** courses requires the participation of line managers as well as the training specialist to ensure that the objectives are clear and the content is appropriate. A typical example of an internal training course would be training employees on a new piece of equipment or machinery in the workplace.

Since **external** courses are usually not designed with a particular organisation in mind, transfer of learning to the workplace may be difficult. External courses usually provide a broad range of knowledge, not all of which may be relevant to participants. One of the strengths of external courses is that they can lead to making contacts with others in the same business. Both internal and external courses can be expensive.

Open or distance learning enables trainees to learn from material prepared and presented elsewhere. The biggest advantage for the trainee is that they can study in their own time, in their own home and at their own pace. Depending on the course, the trainee might have little contact with tutors or other students and will need to be self-motivated and dedicated. These courses are usually quite expensive.

Workshops bring together a group of people who have knowledge or experience of a job with a facilitator who may be a member of the HR department or an outside consultant. This method of training is particularly suitable for managers as it involves active discussion and problem-solving.

Participants often have to do a certain amount of preparation before the workshop takes place. Because the content is relevant, there can be high transfer of learning. Managing a workshop requires a trained facilitator to ensure the effectiveness of the exercise.

E-learning techniques can include computer-based, technology-based and web-based training and learning (Foot and Hook, 2008). E-learning may be used to complement some of the methods already mentioned, such as open or distance learning. Support can be provided by chatrooms, discussion groups and on-line tutoring. Participants can work from home and have a certain amount of flexibility but must have access to the appropriate technology.

> Read through the methods of training again and complete table 5.1.
> Try to think of some more strengths and weaknesses associated with these methods. When you have finished, check your answers with table 5.2 in the summary section of this chapter.

Table 5.1 *Summary of training methods*

Method	Strengths	Weaknesses
Demonstration		
Coaching		
Mentoring		
Job rotation		
Courses		
Open/distance learning		
Workshops		
E-learning		

The evaluation phase

The third stage in the training process involves evaluating whether the training and development was successful or not. It is important that evaluation is carried out to aid future decision-making on whether a particular method should be used again and how it can be implemented most effectively.

> How do you think you could determine whether a training course was effective or not?

Levels of evaluation

Kirkpatrick (1959) suggests that evaluation procedures should consider four levels of criteria:
- reaction
- learning
- behaviour
- results

The simplest way to evaluate a training and development programme is to find out what the participants thought of it. Measuring **reaction** to training is most commonly done by having trainees complete a questionnaire at the end of the training procedure. It is important that the items in a trainee-reaction form should reflect the goals of the training. These data are easy to collect and participant reaction is an important factor when it comes to deciding whether a particular type of training should be repeated. The problem with this level of evaluation is that it does not assess either whether learning actually occurred or whether what was learned was transferred to the workplace. In addition, information collected in this way can be subjective in nature and there is a danger that reaction measures are simply indicators of how much people liked the instructor or enjoyed the course. Enjoyment does not necessarily result in learning, but a training course that participants do not enjoy is unlikely to be repeated often.

The next level of evaluating a training programme is to find out whether participants **learned** any new skills or information. This is done by testing or examining trainees to see what they have learned. It is important that the test relates to the objectives of the training programme. To ensure that learning occurred during training, and not beforehand, it is useful to test trainees before the training as well as after so that results can be compared. Testing is a more objective method of evaluation than measuring the reactions of participants. This method of training evaluation assesses the level of learning that has been achieved but it does not measure transfer of learning. In other words, it does not assess whether skills learned during training are being applied in the workplace and it cannot be assumed that learning always translates into behavioural changes.

The next level of evaluation involves measuring job performance. This can be done by observing the **behaviour** of the trainee in the workplace both before and after training takes place, and either using a checklist for specific job behaviours or using a rating scale to assess to what extent certain job behaviours are evident. Whatever on-the-job performance measures are used, they should be related to the objectives of the training programme. Transfer of learning can be difficult to assess in some jobs.

The final level of evaluation attempts to relate the **results** of the training programme to organisational objectives. Some results that could be examined include costs, turnover, absenteeism, grievances and morale. However, it may not be realistic to link training directly to any of these, as many different factors are often involved.

Unfortunately, the evaluation phase of the development process is often omitted. There are a number of possible reasons to explain why. It is very difficult to evaluate whether training was successful if **training objectives** were not established at the outset. To assess the worth of a particular method, comparisons need to be made between the standards and behaviours before the training and those after. Without the **support of top management** evaluation is often omitted from the process. It is often felt that enough money has been spent on the training itself and that the further **costs** of evaluation are unnecessary. Another reason why evaluation is often ignored is that the trainer may **lack the skills** required to carry out an evaluation. Moreover, evaluating a training and development programme may indicate that it was not effective. The **risk** of such an outcome may prevent evaluation taking place.

Induction Training

Induction is the process of introducing the new employee to their new work environment. Most people are a little anxious on their first day in a new job and it is important that there is a procedure in place to help the new worker become familiar with their surroundings.

Can you remember how you felt on your first day in a new job?

Hill and Trist (1955) found that people are most likely to leave a job in the first few weeks of employment. They called this initial period the 'induction crisis' and thought that the reasons that people were more likely to leave during this time included the job not being what they expected or not liking the job.

Induction training is important because it helps to:
- create a favourable image of the organisation in the mind of the new employee
- lessen anxiety
- reduce misunderstandings
- reduce labour turnover
- achieve performance standards quickly

Have you ever had induction training? If so, what did it consist of?

Induction actually begins before a new employee starts work, as they have started to form an impression of the organisation from information sent to them as well as from the selection process they have completed.

The new employee should receive in written form:
- a description of the organisation
- details of pay and conditions
- a description of duties and responsibilities
- grievance procedures
- disciplinary procedures

In addition, the induction should include:
- a tour of the workplace
- introductions to colleagues and supervisors
- an opportunity for the new employee to ask questions

In the first days and weeks, the new employee should be monitored to make sure that they have settled in and to identify any problems at an early stage.

Summary

The chapter began by discussing the importance of human resource development.
Training and development policy is influenced by:
- management trends
- employment legislation
- the labour market
- available resources

The development process involves three phases:

The preparation phase
- carry out a needs analysis
- set specific goals
- obtain organisational support
- allocate necessary resources
- facilitate transfer of learning

The training–development phase

Table 5.2 *Summary of training methods*

Method	Strengths	Weaknesses
Demonstration	• inexpensive • job relevant • high transfer of learning • trainer knows the job well	• may be time-consuming • trainer may lack training skills • trainee may pick up bad habits
Coaching	• job relevant • trainer knows the job	• may lack structure • pressures of time on supervisor
Mentoring	• learn from experienced manager • useful for succession planning	• requires a lot of manager's time and effort • manager may not have mentoring skills
Job rotation	• inexpensive • trainee sees many aspects of organisation	• may lack structure
Courses	• professional trainers • useful for specific knowledge or skills	• expensive • transfer of learning may be low, especially with external courses • may not be job relevant
Open/distance learning	• flexibility for trainees	• expensive • requires commitment and discipline
Workshops	• job relevant	• requires advance preparation on part of participants
E-learning	• flexibility for trainees	• requires appropriate technology

The evaluation phase
- reaction
- learning
- behaviour
- results

The need for induction training and what should be included in induction training were discussed.

Important Terms and Concepts

available resources
coaching
continuing professional development
cost
courses
demonstration
development
e-learning
employment legislation
evaluation phase
human resource development (HRD)
induction training
job rotation
labour market
learning
learning organisation

levels of evaluation
management trends
mentoring
needs analysis
open or distance learning
organisational support
preparation phase
specific goals
succession planning
support of top management
training
training and development policy
training objectives
training–development phase
transfer of learning
workshops

Revision Questions

1 Discuss the importance of training and development in the organisation.
2 Analyse the factors that influence an organisation's training and development policy.
3 Outline the preparation necessary before training takes place.
4 Evaluate the different methods of training and development.
5 Describe the four levels of evaluation of training and comment on their usefulness.
6 What is the purpose of induction training and what should be included in an induction programme?

6
PERFORMANCE APPRAISAL:
EVALUATING EMPLOYEE PERFORMANCE

Objectives

This chapter will help you to:
- define performance appraisal
- understand the purposes of assessing employee work performance
- identify performance appraisal as part of the HR strategy
- evaluate the different methods of performance appraisal
- distinguish between absolute and relative standards
- discuss the different approaches to the appraisal interview
- consider who should carry out the performance appraisal

Definition

Performance appraisal can be defined as 'a systematic approach to evaluating employees' performance, characteristics or potential with a view to assisting with decisions in a wide range of areas such as pay, promotion, employee development and motivation' (Gunnigle *et al.* 1997, p.145).

Appraisal means **assessment**, and assessing employees' behaviour and achievement of goals is part of the overall system of performance management.

Appraisal takes place every day on an informal basis when supervisors, colleagues and customers observe and evaluate employees in the process of carrying out their duties. Nevertheless, it is important to establish a formal appraisal system that is understood and accepted by those involved.

> Before you read the next section, write down the reasons why you think performance appraisal is carried out.

Purposes of Performance Appraisal

Performance appraisal is part of the overall HR strategy, and information obtained is useful for a number of reasons. It can help to identify **training needs** in cases where employees' performance falls short of the standard required. In addition, it assesses the potential of current employees for future promotion and so aids **succession planning**.

Performance appraisal also provides an opportunity for **two-way feedback** between the manager and the employee. The manager can communicate feedback to the employee regarding their performance at work and the employee can discuss their ambitions within the organisation or any concerns they might have. Goals are clarified and this can have a motivating effect on workers.

Another important purpose of performance appraisal is **documentation**. The results of the appraisal are added to the employee's personnel file having been signed by both the employee and the manager. This information is important if an employee is being considered for either promotion or dismissal.

Sometimes the appraisal is used as an aid to **salary review**. This is not often the case in Ireland as decisions on pay are usually made through collective bargaining.

Think about any previous jobs you may have had.

Was your work ever formally assessed? If so, how?

If not, how do you think performance appraisal is carried out?

Appraisal Methods

In this section the following appraisal methods will be described and evaluated:

1 The essay
2 Critical incident
3 Checklist
4 Rating
5 Ranking
6 Paired comparison
7 Management by objectives (MBO)

Performance appraisal often involves the use of more than one of these methods. Whichever methods are chosen, it is essential when evaluating an employee's work that performance is compared against the requirements outlined in the job description and person specification or competency framework (see chapter two).

1 The essay

The appraiser writes a **free-form narrative** and includes a description of the employee's strengths, weaknesses, potential and areas for improvement. The advantages of this method are that it is simple and flexible. The appraiser does not need any special training to carry out this type of performance evaluation and can include any information that they feel is relevant. It is possible to use great detail which provides qualitative data.

The main drawback is that because there is no structure in this method, it will be difficult to compare employees who have been appraised in this way. In addition, the appraisal may depend on the writing skills of the appraiser. In a large organisation there will be many appraisers, all with different levels of writing skills, thus further confounding the issue of comparison. This method can be subjective, and there is a danger with a free-form appraisal that the appraiser may focus on the employee's personality rather than on their behaviour.

This method is probably most useful in an organisation with few employees, where the same individual carries out all of the appraisals and for jobs where specific job behaviours are difficult to define, such as managerial positions.

2 Critical incident

This method focuses on specific job behaviours. The appraiser keeps a regular account of **incidences of effective and ineffective work behaviours** for each employee and uses these to assess performance. An example of 'good' work behaviour for a cashier might be 'checked gave correct change to customer' and an example of 'bad' work behaviour for a receptionist could be 'didn't give company name when answering the telephone'.

One of the main strengths of this method is that it focuses on job behaviours so performance rather than personality is judged. This makes this type of appraisal more job relevant too. It is easier to give employees either positive or negative feedback based on specific examples of behaviour at work.

A disadvantage of this method is that it is time-consuming for the appraiser to have to write down these incidents on a daily or weekly basis. Good observation skills are required. Moreover, if different examples of good and bad behaviours are identified for each employee, comparison becomes a problem.

This method may be useful in workplaces where it is important that certain procedures are followed, such as health and safety practices on a building site.

3 Checklist

A list of work behaviours relevant to the job is drawn up and the evaluator simply ticks those behaviours that apply to the employee. HRM staff analyse the completed checklist.

Table 6.1 *Sample of checklist items for appraising a sales assistant*

	YES	NO
Does the employee offer to help customers?	____	____
Is the employee courteous to customers?	____	____
Is the employee helpful to other employees?	____	____
Does the employee keep the shelves stocked?	____	____
Does the employee follow shop procedures when accepting payment?	____	____

One of the strengths of this method is that it is job related. In addition, it facilitates comparison of employees. Another advantage is that it is much simpler for the evaluator to tick behaviours than to write an essay-style report on each employee.

However, if there are a number of job categories in the organisation, a checklist has to be made out for each one and this can be time-consuming.

Like the critical incident method, the checklist method can be useful when specific behaviours of the job can be identified as being essential.

4 Rating

This method requires the use of a scale on which certain behaviours or characteristics are listed. The appraiser decides to what degree the employee exhibits the behaviours or possesses the characteristics, for example from poor to excellent.

Table 6.2 *Sample of rating scale for appraising a sales assistant*

Main duties	1	2	3	4	5	Comments
Assisting customers						
Cooperating with other employees						
Stocking shelves						
Dealing with complaints						
Dealing with suppliers						
Rating scale: 1 Poor, 2 Satisfactory, 3 Good, 4 Very good, 5 Excellent						

This is a popular method of performance appraisal perhaps due to the fact that it is very convenient for the appraiser to use. In addition, it is easy to make comparisons among employees.

However, it can be difficult to measure personality or behavioural traits on a rating scale. Moreover, there is a danger with some rating scales that users might simply choose the middle value for all appraisees. This is called the 'error of central tendency' and can be reduced by using certain rating scales, such as **the forced choice technique**, which do not have a middle value.

The four appraisal methods described above have something in common: each of these methods uses **absolute standards**. This means that the method itself does not involve comparison with any other person. Each employee is evaluated on their own merits. In the cases of the checklist and rating, it is possible to compare employees afterwards. However, employees can also be appraised against **relative standards**. These methods involve comparison of workers as part of the evaluation process and will be examined next.

5 Ranking

Ranking means putting in order. A soldier's rank indicates their position in the army hierarchy in order of importance. In the workplace employees can be ranked from best to worst. The **individual ranking method** requires the appraiser to list the employees in order from highest to lowest. The **group**

order ranking method requires the evaluator to place employees into a particular classification such as 'top quarter', 'second quarter' and so on.

The main advantages of this appraisal method are that it is easy to carry out and that it facilitates the comparison of employees.

However, with a small number of workers who are all very good, some will have to be placed in the 'last quarter' and this may give a misleading picture of these workers' performances. Another problem with ranking is that the degrees of difference are not specified. This means that there may only be a tiny difference between the first and second worker and then a bigger gap between the second and third. Ranking can be difficult to carry out where large numbers of employees are involved.

6 Paired comparison

This method involves comparing each worker to every other worker. Two workers are compared at a time and a decision is made as to who is superior. Each employee is given a score which depends on the number of times the individual is the preferred member. Finally all employees are ranked. This is often seen as a more comprehensive and fairer way of ranking employees but of course the weaknesses of ranking, as mentioned above, apply here too.

To help illustrate the difference between absolute and relative standards, take the example of student assessment. When a student's essay or examination is marked, it receives an absolute mark of, for example, 60 per cent. This mark is arrived at by evaluating the essay or exam on its own merits. A clearer assessment of the student involves comparing their performance to the rest of the class. Assessing the student against relative standards means assessing how their mark compares with the marks of the other students in the class.

7 Management by objectives (MBO)

This method of evaluating employee performance involves assessing the extent to which job objectives are achieved. Objectives are derived from the organisation's strategic plan and cascaded down to departments and individual employees. The process involves the manager and employee agreeing a number of objectives to be achieved by the employee for a particular period. Examples of objectives may include increasing sales by 5 per cent, improving the quality of the product or service, increasing production, reducing bad debts and reducing customer complaints. A number of interim reviews take place between the manager and the employee to determine how well the objectives are being achieved. It may be necessary to amend objectives if business circumstances have changed.

One of the main advantages of MBO is that assessment of performance is based on specific objectives. Moreover, employees have greater direction and control over their work, which can lead to greater motivation, and ultimately greater overall organisation performance. MBO also contributes towards improved interpersonal relationships between manager and employee due to the increase in communication.

The disadvantages sometimes associated with the MBO appraisal method are that the process may become bureaucratic and time-consuming for the manager. Furthermore, employees may only concentrate on those goals that will be rewarded and may neglect other responsibilities.

> For a summary of the appraisal methods discussed above, see table 6.3 in the summary section of this chapter.

The Appraisal Interview

Most performance appraisal processes involve an appraisal interview as part of the process. The appraisal interview tends to follow one of **three interviewing styles**:

- tell-and-sell
- tell-and-listen
- problem-solving

The **tell-and-sell** method begins when the appraisee is told the results of their appraisal. The manager then gets their acceptance of the evaluation and tells them how to improve. When this approach is used, the employee has little involvement in the appraisal process. It may be appropriate in situations where workers have very little experience and need direction.

The **tell-and-listen** approach also begins with the result of the appraisal being communicated to the employee. It differs from the tell-and-sell method in that the appraisee is encouraged to respond to the evaluation results.

The **problem-solving** style is completely different. The appraiser does not act as a judge as in the previous two approaches. In fact the appraisal result is not communicated to the employee at this stage. Instead, the employee is encouraged to discuss any difficulties in their work situation and to consider the solutions. The final evaluation takes place **as a result of** the interview.

> Before you read the next section, think about a job you have/had. Make
> a list of the people in a position to evaluate your work.

Contributors to the Appraisal Process

Most appraisals are carried out by the employee's **immediate supervisor** or
manager. They may not get to see every detail of how the employee carries out
tasks, but they see the end result of the employee's performance such as
whether sales targets were reached or deadlines were met.

Colleagues are often asked to evaluate each other's work performance. This
is called **peer assessment**. Colleagues may be in a better position to judge, as
they see the actual behaviour of their co-workers on a day-to-day basis as they
carry out tasks and interact with customers. Research has shown that this form
of assessment can be reliable (Latham and Wexley, 1981). It is not commonly
used, however, perhaps because employees feel uncomfortable about
assessing other workers and also because employees may react badly to peer
appraisal and be more likely to accept the appraisal of a superior.

Customers are a useful source of appraisal information. This is done by
analysing comment cards and customer complaints. 'Secret shoppers' are used
to assess the techniques used by sales staff, for instance.

Subordinates are a potential source of appraisal information too. Information
from subordinates may be limited in value as they may not know much about the
work done by their superior. It can be useful in evaluating management style,
however. It is not frequently used, probably because workers feel uncomfortable
about assessing a superior, and managers may find it harder to accept these
evaluations. It may interfere with the authority a manager has over subordinates.

Employees can evaluate themselves and are often asked to do so as part of
the appraisal process and in preparation for the appraisal interview. All of the
methods mentioned are open to bias and **self-appraisal** is no exception.

360-degree appraisal

360-degree feedback or **multi-rater assessment** involves collecting
information from all of the sources mentioned above. When external sources
such as customers and suppliers are included, it is sometimes called 540-
degree feedback. This type of appraisal provides information on different
aspects of the employee's performance, giving a rounded view of the
individual's strengths and weaknesses. However, it can be difficult to gather

information from so many sources. In addition, this method is time-consuming and can be expensive.

Summary

The purposes of performance appraisal are to:
- identify training needs
- aid succession planning
- provide two-way feedback
- provide documentation
- aid salary review

Table 6.3 *Summary of appraisal methods*

Method	Strengths	Weaknesses
Essay	• easy to use • flexible	• no structure • difficult to compare employees • can be subjective • time-consuming to carry out
Critical incident	• focus on job behaviours	• time-consuming to construct • difficult to compare employees
Checklist	• easy to use • job related • easy comparison	• time-consuming to construct
Rating	• easy to use • easy comparison	• not suitable for all characteristics • error of central tendency • time-consuming to construct
Ranking	• easy to use • easy comparison	• degrees of difference not specified • difficult with large numbers
Paired comparison	• easy to use • more comprehensive approach than ranking	• same as for ranking
Management by objectives	• specific objectives set • motivates employees • improves communication	• time-consuming • can be bureaucratic • employees may neglect other duties

Styles of appraisal interview:
- tell-and-sell
- tell-and-listen
- problem-solving

Contributors to the appraisal process:
- immediate supervisor
- peer assessment
- customers
- subordinates
- self-appraisal
- 360-degree appraisal

Important Terms and Concepts

absolute standards

appraisal interview

checklist

critical incident

customers

documentation

essay-type appraisal

free-form narrative

group order ranking method

immediate supervisor

individual ranking method

management by objectives

multi-rater assessment

paired comparison

peer assessment

performance appraisal

problem-solving interview

ranking

rating

relative standards

salary review

self-appraisal

subordinates

succession planning

tell-and-listen

tell-and-sell

360-degree appraisal or feedback

training needs

two-way feedback

Revision Questions

1 Outline the main purposes of a performance appraisal.
2 How is the performance appraisal linked to the HR strategy?
3 Distinguish between absolute and relative standards.
4 Evaluate the methods of performance appraisal.
5 Describe the different approaches to the appraisal interview.
6 Discuss the potential contributors to the appraisal process.

7
MOTIVATING EMPLOYEES

Objectives

This chapter will help you to:
- define motivation
- understand the link between motivation and HRM
- distinguish between content and process theories of motivation
- discuss workers' needs and how they can be met by the organisation
- explain the importance of the work environment and job design in relation to employee motivation
- discuss the influence of equity theory on worker motivation
- examine the role of goal-setting in motivation

Definition

Steers and Porter (1991) define motivation as 'the set of forces that cause people to behave in certain ways'.

When a murder is committed, detectives look for a **motive** for the killing. They want to know what **caused** the murderer to commit the crime. They want to know **the reason why**. Theories of work motivation attempt to understand why people behave the way they do at work. These theories try to explain why some people work very hard, for example, and why some employees try to get away with doing as little as possible.

Motivation and HRM

You may remember from chapter one that the human resource style of management views employees as a **valuable resource**. 'Soft' HRM recognises **individual differences** among employees and concentrates on nurturing and developing staff as a means of achieving corporate aims. A knowledge and understanding of human motivation is essential for **effective human resource management**. It is helpful when dealing with problems such as **absenteeism**, **employee turnover**, low **morale** and low **quality** or **productivity**. The concepts of employee motivation can be usefully applied in strategies for effective **reward management** (see chapter eight). According to Pettinger

(1994) there is a correlation between organisations that go to a lot of trouble to motivate their staff and profitable business performance.

Applying Motivation Theory

Theories of motivation can be divided into two types. **Content** or **needs theories** focus on identifying *what* motivates people. Things that can motivate people include money, job security, prestige and the need for achievement. Maslow (1943), McGregor (1960), Alderfer (1972) and McClelland (1961) are among those whose theories fit into this category. Other theories focus on *how* the process of motivation takes place. Examples of these **process theories** include expectancy theory, goal-setting theory and Adams' equity theory (1963).

Drawing information from a number of theories, this chapter summarises some of the issues that a manager needs to consider when dealing with problems of motivation in the workplace:

1 Meeting employees' basic needs
2 Helping employees to reach their full potential
3 Choosing rewards that employees value
4 Providing a suitable work environment
5 Looking at how jobs are designed
6 Ensuring that employees feel fairly treated
7 Setting goals

The next two sections discuss the link between workers' needs and motivation. As you read, think about jobs you have had and to what extent your needs were satisfied.

---

1 Meeting employees' basic needs

Some theorists believe that **identifying workers' needs** is the key to motivation. If a manager knows what an employee needs, relevant incentives can be offered in return for hard work, reduced absenteeism and so on.

Maslow's '**hierarchy of needs**' is a popular theory of motivation. It identifies five levels of needs that an individual may have and assumes that people want to work their way up the levels to reach their fullest potential.

The most basic level in Maslow's hierarchy represents **physiological needs**. These are the things needed to survive and include air, food, water, sunlight and rest. Most workers expect these needs to be met in the workplace in the form of a basic salary, a canteen, adequate ventilation and rest breaks.

In fact, organisations have a legal responsibility to provide their employees with these basic needs. For example, the Safety, Health and Welfare at Work (Miscellaneous Welfare Provisions) Regulations (1995) outline the employer's duty to provide drinking water and facilities for taking meals, the National Minimum Wage Act (2000) provides for basic pay and the Organisation of Working Time Act (1997) specifies the legislation regarding rest breaks. See chapter eleven for more information on employment legislation.

According to Maslow's theory, once an individual's physiological needs have been taken care of they become less important and the individual now focuses on **safety needs**. People want to feel secure in their work environment and the organisation can cater for these needs by offering contracts and permanent positions as well as pension plans, health insurance and a safe working environment. These two levels of Maslow's theory correspond with **existence needs** in Alderfer's **ERG theory**.

Employers are legally obliged to provide a safe and secure work environment for employees. See the Terms of Employment (Information) Acts (1994 and 2001), the Safety, Health and Welfare at Work Acts (1989 and 2005) and the Pensions (Amendment) Act (2002).

The next level of needs is **belongingness**. This corresponds to McClelland's **need for affiliation** and Alderfer's **relatedness need**. Everybody, to some extent, has the need for friendship, to be liked by colleagues and to fit in at work. The organisation can help to facilitate the satisfaction of this need by encouraging teamwork, organising office parties and assisting in the setting up of social clubs.

Although Maslow felt that workers would be motivated to satisfy their physiological and safety needs, another theorist, Herzberg (1966), disagreed. His research led him to the conclusion that two completely different sets of factors exist. The first set of factors is called **'hygiene' factors** and these correspond to the lower levels of Maslow's hierarchy. Herzberg felt that workers are not actually motivated by pay and security and other lower order needs, but that they will be very dissatisfied if they do not have enough of them. So, according to this theory, providing for a worker's basic needs can prevent dissatisfaction at work but will not lead to motivation. Herzberg's second set of factors will be discussed later.

Employee needs can be identified at various stages of the employment relationship. For example, both the selection and the appraisal interviews can be used to find out what motivates employees. In addition, information can be collected during everyday interactions with staff.

2 Helping employees to reach their full potential

Humanistic psychologists believe that we all have an innate desire to be the best that we can be. They believe that we become unhappy and frustrated if we are prevented from reaching our fullest potential.

The fourth level in Maslow's hierarchy is esteem. This refers to workers' needs for confidence, recognition and respect in their jobs. **Esteem needs** can be met by the employer in the form of 'employee of the month' awards, promotion, a bigger office or better job title. Giving more responsibility and placing value on the individual's advice or suggestions can also satisfy esteem needs.

Self-actualisation is the final level in Maslow's hierarchy of needs. The organisation can help employees to reach their fullest potential by providing opportunities for promotion, encouraging creativity and setting challenging work assignments.

The final levels of Maslow's theory correspond to Herzberg's second set of factors, which he called '**motivating factors**'. He believed that workers are motivated to satisfy these higher level needs. McGregor's **Theory Y** also proposes the view that people are ambitious, enjoy work and want responsibility. Alderfer referred to the higher levels of needs as **growth needs**.

According to Maslow, though, a particular level of needs does not motivate individuals until the ones before it have been satisfied. If this is the case, an employee will not be motivated to earn more respect and prestige at work if the basic needs have not been met.

Alderfer on the other hand believed that while an individual could get enough of the lower level needs and not want to get any more of those basic things, higher level needs are never satisfied. This implies that an employee can always be motivated to satisfy esteem and self-actualisation needs. If this is the case, it is essential for a manager to recognise the importance of higher order needs. Needs can be identified by using interviews or questionnaires.

3 Choosing rewards that employees value

A manager cannot assume that every worker will be motivated by the same incentives. A lot depends on how much value an employee places on certain things. **Expectancy theory** predicts that workers are motivated by pay and other rewards only if the employee values these rewards. This is called **valence**. This theory suggests that rather than identifying the level of needs a worker is focusing on, a manager should try to identify what the employee values. This could be money, free time or more responsibility, for example.

Alderfer thought that a person could be motivated by more than one need at any particular time. For example, a worker may try to satisfy a basic need such as earning enough money to survive and at the same time focus on a higher level need such as recognition for work done. The organisation should facilitate good performance by providing adequate opportunities for employees to satisfy their varying needs.

4 Providing a suitable work environment

McClelland is another theorist who believed that an individual could be trying to satisfy a number of needs at the same time. He studied the need for achievement (**nAch**), the need for affiliation (**nAff**) and the need for autonomy (**nAut**). He proposed that a person could have different levels of each of these needs. In order to motivate workers, it is necessary to measure these needs and then provide **appropriate work environments**.

People with a high need for achievement work best in challenging work environments. They also need feedback on work performance. Those with a high need for affiliation have a strong need for approval and reassurance from others. They tend to choose jobs high in interpersonal contact and work best in a supportive, cooperative work environment. Employees with a high need for autonomy find it hard to work when there are too many rules and regulations. They often prefer to work alone and like to control the pace of their work. A manager can use McClelland's work to get the best performance from workers either by employing employees most suited to the existing work environment or by providing an appropriate work environment for existing employees.

Table 7.1 *An overview of content/needs theories of motivation*

Maslow's hierarchy	Alderfer's ERG	Herzberg	McClelland
Self-actualisation	Growth		Autonomy
Esteem		Motivating factors	Achievement
Belongingness	Relatedness		Affiliation
Safety	Existence	Hygiene factors	
Physiological			

5 Looking at how jobs are designed

Job design is how an organisation defines and structures jobs. Several writers have tackled the area of job design (see Armstrong, 2001) and suggest characteristics which have an important effect on employee motivation. Ideally, jobs should be designed in such a way that employees:

- are responsible for a complete piece of work, or at least a significant part of it, so that they can recognise a whole product as the result of their work
- have the opportunity to use a variety of skills
- feel that their work is important
- are responsible for setting goals and deciding how their work will be carried out
- monitor their own performance and progress
- receive constructive feedback on their performance

It is also worth considering flexible working arrangements such as flexitime, job sharing, part-time contracts, home-working and sabbaticals.

6 Ensuring that employees feel fairly treated

Adams' **equity theory** of motivation contends that motivation at work is influenced by *perceived* fairness in the workplace. Employees assess what they bring to their jobs and what they get in return and they compare this to what other workers put in and get back. Examples of what people bring to their jobs include experience, qualifications, effort and time. Pay, experience, contacts and recognition are some of the things they get in return.

If workers feel unfairly treated in comparison to others, they will be motivated to restore equity in the situation. Behaviours in reaction to perceived inequity include asking for a pay rise, making less effort or leaving the job.

Managers have to be aware that this type of comparison exists and of the potential negative consequences to the organisation if workers feel unfairly treated. What a manager believes to be fair is irrelevant if employees perceive the situation to be inequitable. Employees behave in reaction to their own perception of the situation, not that of the manager. It is important that managers ensure that employees feel equitably treated.

7 Setting goals

Setting targets is another way to try to motivate employees. Earlier in the chapter it was noted that people with a high need for achievement work best in a challenging work environment. Humanistic psychologists such as Maslow and Rogers believe that all people have a natural desire to reach their fullest potential and be the best that they can be.

These theorists believe that **goal setting** is healthy both for the worker and for the organisation. A manager needs to be concerned about how high these targets are set. Do employees feel that the goals provide them with enough of a challenge? Are the targets attainable? If the targets are set too low some workers may not feel challenged enough and will not make much effort. On the other hand, it is not advisable to set targets too high either. **Expectancy theory** predicts that an individual will not be motivated if they cannot see a link between their effort and achievement of the target. In other words, if a worker feels that the goal is impossible to reach no matter how much effort is made, motivation will be reduced. Targets need to be achievable.

Summary

When confronted with motivational problems in the workplace a manager needs to consider:
- the needs of employees
- what employees place value on
- the work environment
- job design
- whether people feel fairly treated at work
- goal setting

Important Terms and Concepts

absenteeism
belongingness
content/needs theories
effective human resource
   management
employee turnover
equity theory
ERG theory
esteem needs
existence needs
expectancy theory
goal setting
growth needs
hierarchy of needs
hygiene factors

identifying workers' needs
individual differences
job design
morale
motivating factors
motivation
nAch
nAff
nAut
physiological needs
process theories
relatedness needs
safety needs
self-actualisation
valence

Revision Questions

1 Explain why knowledge of motivation theory is so important in human resource management.
2 Distinguish between content and process theories of motivation.
3 Discuss the needs identified by Maslow and others. How do they influence motivation?
4 What advice would you give to a manager who is having problems motivating staff?

8
REWARD MANAGEMENT

Objectives

This chapter will help you to:
- define reward management
- explain why reward management is important
- identify reward management as part of the overall HR strategy
- discuss the factors that influence pay levels
- understand the different methods of job evaluation
- outline the different elements of the reward package
- evaluate the different payment systems available to employers
- describe the essential characteristics of a reward package

Definition

Gunnigle and Flood (1990, p.114) state that 'managing rewards involves the establishment and maintenance of adequate remuneration systems which attract, retain and motivate the organisation's workforce in line with business objectives'.

The Importance of Reward Management

The decisions made regarding pay and benefits play a role in achieving human resource management outcomes and objectives by:
- **attracting** potential employees
- **retaining** good employees
- **motivating** employees

Reward management, therefore, is linked to other aspects of the human resource role in an organisation such as planning, recruitment, training and motivation. The resulting HR strategies should complement organisational objectives, for instance gaining competitive advantage and increasing levels of job satisfaction.

Factors that Influence Pay Levels

> Think about the payment you received for doing a particular job. Why do you think you were paid this amount and not more or less?

The main factors influencing pay levels are:
1   Economic climate
2   Labour market
3   Legislation
4   Trade union and employee demands
5   Benchmarking

1 Economic climate

In times of **economic prosperity**, workers and trade unions often put pressure on employers to increase their pay. In fact, the number of industrial disputes and strikes increases when the economy is doing well. This is because organisations are making more money and employees want to make sure they get some of it. There is little point in pushing for a pay rise during an economic recession when there is no money available. Another economic factor is **inflation**. When inflation levels are high, prices go up and workers look for pay increases to match the cost of living.

Inflation and economic prosperity influence **what an organisation can afford** to pay. This is probably one of the first factors that the organisation should consider before making an offer to employees. Moreover, economic factors influence what **other organisations** can pay. In an effort to recruit the best employees, an organisation might choose to pay a little more than the going rate.

2 Labour market

The **availability of workers** in the labour market influences pay levels. If an organisation is having difficulty recruiting workers in general, or workers with **specific skills or qualifications**, they may have to offer a better rewards package to attract people. In recent years people with specialised IT skills could command large salaries and fringe benefits. However, if the supply of workers or skills is greater than the demand for them, the organisation is in a position to be less generous. For this reason, unskilled workers have less bargaining power when it comes to decisions on pay.

3 Legislation

The main legislation that affects reward systems in Irish organisations is: the **National Minimum Wage Act (2000)**, which, with some exceptions, means that employees are guaranteed at least €8.65 per hour from 1 July 2007.

The **Employment Equality Acts (1998–2008)** state that employees must be paid the same for like work and cannot be discriminated against on the basis of sex, age, disability, marital status, family status, sexual orientation, race, religion or membership of the Travelling community.

Employment legislation is covered in more detail in chapter eleven.

4 Trade union and employee demands

When the economy is doing well and there is low unemployment, workers, often represented by trade unions, are in a relatively powerful position. The demands of individual workers or collective bargaining by unions can result in pay increases. In fact, there have been times when unions were so successful in negotiating pay deals that they were accused of causing inflation. However, employee bargaining power is reduced in times of economic recession.

5 Benchmarking

Job benchmarking is a major review of a particular job's pay, benefits, skills, perks, demands, responsibilities and other conditions compared to a similar post in a different sector. The Irish government's benchmarking body conducted a study which compared the work conditions of 230,000 public servants (including clerical and administration workers, nurses, gardaí, civil servants, prison officers and teachers) with similar jobs in the private sector. The main purpose of the benchmarking process was to decide pay levels for public sector workers. Most trade unions and employer associations cooperated with the process and made submissions, representing members' views, to the benchmarking body. The report was published on 1 July 2002 and its findings received mixed reactions from different interested parties.

Job Evaluation

Job evaluation involves assessing the value of the job to the organisation and it leads to decisions on how much each employee should be paid.

Armstrong (2009, p.740) defines job evaluation as 'a systematic process for establishing the relative worth of jobs within an organisation'.

> Before you read on, consider the following questions:
> Think of an organisation you know. Why do different employees get paid different amounts?
> Think about different jobs. Why does a professional footballer get paid so much? Why does a computer programmer earn more than a receptionist?

This section describes the main methods of evaluating jobs:
1 Job ranking
2 Paired comparison
3 Job classification
4 Points rating
5 The Hay Method
6 Competence-based job evaluation

1 *Job ranking*

Ranking means 'placing in a hierarchy'. This method of job evaluation involves placing jobs in order of importance or value to the organisation. Whole jobs are compared, which means that the jobs are not broken down into components, such as qualifications required or amount of responsibility involved. Once the jobs have been ranked, they are arranged into groups or grades. Finally, pay levels are agreed for each grade.

Job ranking is a straightforward way of evaluating jobs. It is easy to understand and quick and inexpensive to operate. This method is probably most useful in organisations with small numbers of jobs.

One of the weaknesses of job ranking is that it is subjective. This means that it is possible that different people will rank jobs in different orders. Since standards for ranking are not defined, it may be difficult to justify why jobs are put in a particular order. Another limitation is that this method of job evaluation is not analytical. In other words, the job is considered as a whole, and factors such as skills, responsibility and working conditions are not taken into account. This makes it difficult to justify pay differences following job evaluation. Finally, ranking is difficult where large numbers of jobs are involved.

> Make a list of all of the jobs in an organisation you know. Now rank them in order starting with the one you think is **most important or valuable** to the organisation. Do not consider elements of the job, such as qualifications required. Now decide a grading structure for these jobs. Jobs within a particular grade will merit the same pay.

2 Paired comparison

This method of job evaluation is a more systematic version of ranking. A list of jobs is compiled and each job is compared to every other job. Points are scored on the basis of each comparison. Whichever of the two jobs is more valuable receives two points. If it is decided that the jobs are of equal value, they get one point each. The job that is worth less gets no points. When each job has been compared to every other job, the points are added. Now the jobs are ranked in order from the most points to the least, suggesting the jobs in order of their value to the organisation.

Paired comparison is a more systematic and comprehensive approach to job evaluation than simple job ranking. Apart from this, both methods share similar advantages and disadvantages.

3 Job classification

Job classification is similar to job ranking but uses a different approach. Using the job classification system, the number of pay grades is decided first, for example grades one to five. This grading structure is based on differences in skill, qualifications, responsibility and so on. Jobs are then placed into these grades. As with job ranking, the jobs are not broken down into components but are assessed as a whole.

This method of job evaluation is easy to operate. By first deciding on a grading structure, some standards for ranking are defined, and it will be easy to fit new jobs into the classification structure once it has been established. Job classification is suitable for dealing with large numbers of employees.

However, job classification becomes complicated when there is a wide range of jobs to evaluate. Some jobs may not fit neatly into one grade only.

4 Points rating

This commonly used method of job evaluation involves breaking down each job into a number of job factors. Benge (1944) suggested the following:
- skill requirements
- responsibility
- physical requirements
- mental requirements
- working conditions

Points are allocated for each element of the job and totalled.

The points rating method of job evaluation is more objective than job ranking or job classification. It is also analytical, which means that the job is broken down into components for evaluation purposes. Because standards of comparison are clearly defined, it is easier to explain differences in pay following job evaluation.

A disadvantage of the points rating method is that it is more complex than job ranking or job classification. It is also more time-consuming and costly to develop. Moreover, even though this method of job evaluation is more objective than the others discussed so far in this chapter, it still relies on subjective judgement to some extent.

5 The Hay Method

The Hay Method is widely used and is traditionally associated with evaluating managerial and professional jobs. The method relies on three main factors:

- know-how
- problem-solving
- accountability

Each of these factors is further subdivided and points are allocated based on comparisons made among jobs.

The Hay Method is more objective than many other approaches, and this contributes to its wide acceptance. The main drawback lies in its complexity. In addition, this method of job evaluation is time-consuming and expensive to develop. A certain amount of subjective judgement is required.

6 Competence-based job evaluation

With this type of job evaluation the emphasis is on an evaluation of the *person* who performs the job and their competence and performance abilities rather than on the job title or grade. The following are considered important:

- interpersonal skills
- communication skills
- technical knowledge
- decision-making ability
- teamworking and leadership skills

The key strength of competence-based or skill-based job evaluation is that this approach focuses on the person rather than on the job. However, a criticism of this method is that there may be too much emphasis on the individual's skills and knowledge and not enough on how productive the job is. Another drawback is the complexity of the approach.

Read through the section on methods of job evaluation again and complete table 8.1. Check your answers against table 8.2 in the summary section of this chapter.

Table 8.1 *Summary of strengths and weaknesses of job evaluation methods*

Method	Strengths	Weaknesses
Job ranking		
Paired comparison		
Job classification		
Points rating		
The Hay Method		
Competence-based job evaluation		

The Reward Package

Reward management involves making decisions about the amount and the form of payment employees should receive.

The main elements of a reward package are:
- **pay**, which refers to the basic wage or salary
- **incentives**, which are rewards for performance beyond normal expectations
- **benefits**, also known as indirect pay, which include pensions and health insurance

Pay, incentives and benefits combine in a number of ways to form different types of payment systems.

> Before you read the next section, think about how you were paid for jobs you have done.
> Did you get paid by the hour, week or month?
> Were you guaranteed pay increases for length of service?
> Did all employees receive the same rewards regardless of effort and productivity, or were bonuses and commission used to motivate employees to work harder?
> Were you guaranteed an income, or did pay depend wholly on results?
> Did you share in the organisation's profits?
> Was your pay based on your skills and qualifications?

Payment Systems

Systems for paying employees include:
- flat-rate pay
- incremental pay scale
- incentive pay
- payment by results
- performance-related pay
- gainsharing
- competence or skill-based pay

The **flat-rate** system is the traditional approach to payment: people are paid according to the time they spend at work. Pay can be calculated on an hourly, weekly or annual basis. This system provides stable earnings for employees and the payroll is easy to organise. It is also useful when performance criteria are difficult to establish. A potential problem is that if everyone is paid the same then there is no incentive for employees to work harder.

An **incremental pay scale** is a form of the flat-rate system where employees are paid for the time they spend at work but are guaranteed an extra amount or increment every year. This system is designed to encourage employees to stay with the same organisation for a long period of time. Incremental pay schemes are generally accepted as fair as they tend to be based on length of service. It usually takes a few years to work your way up the scale, which might be frustrating for ambitious workers, and once you reach the top of the scale there is little incentive to work hard any more. This payment system is common in large bureaucratic organisations.

Incentive pay systems involve making a payment, in addition to the flat rate, based on performance. This extra payment can be based on an individual employee's performance or on the performance of a group, such as a sales team. While this approach can be good for motivation and is useful when it is difficult to measure individual performance, it can cause harmful competition within the organisation. Examples include **bonuses** and **commission**.

Individual payment by results is a system where the amount that a person is paid depends on the amount they produce. The employee is not paid for the time it took to complete the job but instead for its completion. Also known as **piecework**, this approach is best used in work environments such as factories where it is easy to measure the quantity of work completed. This pay system provides an incentive to increase effort and decrease the amount of time taken to do the job. However, it makes organising the payroll more complicated and there is a danger that quality may suffer. It is often seen as an unacceptable system as there is no guarantee of an income.

Performance-related pay, also known as **merit rating**, is used as an incentive in situations where the actual work rate is difficult to measure. Assessing employees' performance fairly is difficult to do and this is the main reason that trade unions tend to oppose performance-related pay. In order for this approach to be effective, it is important that employees are involved in setting up the system and that performance criteria are clearly defined.

Gainsharing is an approach to reward management that involves rewarding employees for the organisation's success. It can take the form of **profit-sharing** where employees are promised a bonus when the organisation makes a profit. Another example is **share ownership** where employees are given shares in the company. This form of payment system is used to encourage cooperation between management and workers (remember the concept of unitarism in chapter one?) and increase commitment to the organisation. The problem is that employees may find it difficult to see a link between their own individual performance and that of the organisation.

Competence or skill-based payment systems focus on the worker's level of skill rather than on the job itself. There is a basic rate of pay for having the minimum level of skill and employees will be paid more if they have or acquire new skills that assist them in their jobs. This approach encourages employees to continuously update their skills and qualifications.

Another element of the rewards package incorporates **non-monetary rewards**. These **benefits** include extra holiday time, health insurance, sick pay and pensions – none of which an employer is obliged to provide.

Essential Characteristics of a Reward System

Lawler (1977) outlined five '**essential characteristics**' of an effective reward system. These elements should be considered when putting a reward package together:

- reward level
- individuality
- internal equity
- external equity
- trust

Employees' needs were discussed in chapter seven. The **reward level** offered must be enough to live on as well as to satisfy the employees' other basic needs such as security and esteem. The minimum reward level has been determined by legislation. Because the cost of living is higher in Dublin, for example, employers often have to offer higher basic salaries than are paid for similar jobs in other parts of the country.

The reward system should be able to provide for the **individuality** of employees and be flexible enough to meet their different needs. The concept of valence, discussed in chapter seven, recognises that different employees value different things. Some organisations offer a choice of fringe benefits so that employees can choose, for example, between a pension contribution and extra holiday time. This is known as the '**cafeteria approach**'; a flexible pay system that allows employees to choose their own reward or combination of rewards. The concept of individuality is also linked to **performance-related pay**. Decisions have to be made as to whether all employees will receive the same rewards or whether rewards should depend on effort or results.

It is important to remember that workers compare themselves to other workers in the organisation. This is the main point of Adams' equity theory (chapter seven). Employees want to feel fairly treated when they consider what they put into their jobs and what they get in return. It is essential that workers perceive **internal equity** in the pay system devised by the organisation. A transparent reward system with clearly explained differentials is necessary.

Employees also compare themselves to workers in other similar organisations. Again, they want to feel fairly treated in comparison with what is being offered elsewhere.

It is important that the pay systems of competing organisations are analysed when a pay system is being designed. Workers need to perceive **external equity**. One of the reasons for a shortage of nurses in Ireland in the 2000s was that many nurses chose to work in the pharmaceutical industry where they could earn more money and have better working conditions.

The final characteristic described by Lawler is **trust**. Employees need to believe that rewards will be given for work done and targets achieved. In addition, management must trust that employees will work to the level expected of them in order to get these rewards.

> To what extent do Lawler's essential characteristics apply to your own work experiences?

Summary

Good reward management is necessary for attracting, retaining and motivating staff and is part of the overall HR strategy.

The payment system in an organisation is influenced by:
- economic climate
- labour market
- legislation
- trade unions
- benchmarking

The main methods of job evaluation are:

Table 8.2 *Summary of strengths and weaknesses of job evaluation methods*

Method	Strengths	Weaknesses
Job ranking	• straightforward • easily understood • quick and cheap to operate • useful with small numbers of jobs	• subjective • no defined standards • difficult with large numbers • not analytical: job seen as a whole
Paired comparison	• same as for job ranking but more systematic	• same as for job ranking
Job classification	• easy to operate • provides some standards • suitable for large numbers of employees • easy to fit new jobs into classification	• difficult with wide number of jobs • job may not fit into one grade only • job considered as a whole
Points rating	• more objective than above methods • analytical: job broken into components • helps to explain differences in pay • standards of comparison clearly defined	• more complex than above methods • time-consuming to develop • costly to develop • still relies on subjective judgement
The Hay Method	• objective • widely accepted	• complex • time-consuming to develop • costly • still relies on subjective opinion
Competence-based job evaluation	• focus on person rather than job	• too much emphasis on skills • not enough emphasis on output • complex

The rewards package contains a mixture of pay, incentives and benefits in the form of:

• flat-rate pay
• incremental pay
• incentive pay
• payment by results

- performance-related pay
- gainsharing
- competence or skill-based pay

Non-monetary rewards include:
- pension
- health insurance
- paid sick leave
- extra holiday time

Lawler's essential characteristics are:
- reward level
- individuality
- internal equity
- external equity
- trust

Important Terms and Concepts

attract employees	job evaluation
benchmarking	job ranking
benefits	labour market
bonus	merit rating
cafeteria approach	motivating employees
commission	National Minimum Wage Act (2000)
competence-based job evaluation	paired comparison
competence-based payment	pay
economic climate	payment by results
Employment Equality Acts (1998–2008)	performance-related pay
	piecework
flat rate	points rating
gainsharing	profit-sharing
Hay Method	retain employees
incentives	reward level
incremental pay scale	reward management
individuality	reward package
inflation	share ownership
internal/external equity	trade unions
job classification	

Revision Questions

1 Explain why reward management is an important part of the overall HR strategy.
2 Discuss the factors that influence the composition of the reward package.
3 Describe the different methods of job evaluation.
4 Analyse the 'essential characteristics' of the reward system as described by Lawler (1977).
5 Outline the different elements of the reward package.

SECTION 4

EMPLOYMENT RELATIONS

Chapter 9 Trade Unions and Employers' Associations
Chapter 10 Dispute Resolution
Chapter 11 Employment Legislation

Think about a place where you have worked. How would you describe the relationship between workers and management? To what extent is the relationship affected by:

- the workers themselves and the trade unions that represent them?
- the employers?
- the way grievances and disputes are dealt with?
- employment law?

Employment relations refers to the relationship between workers and management. The term 'employment relations' is used instead of '**industrial relations**', which in the past was more commonly used to describe the trade union–management relationship in blue collar organisations. Employment relations has a broader meaning encompassing non-union and service sector organisations. Employment relations are said to be good when there is harmony between managers and employees in the workplace. Employment relations are poor when there is conflict in the form of grievances or disputes.

This section of the book examines the role of workers and employers in the employment relationship. In addition, both organisational and state dispute-resolution facilities are discussed. Finally, the role of employment legislation in regulating the employment relationship is addressed.

9
TRADE UNIONS AND EMPLOYERS' ASSOCIATIONS

Objectives

This chapter will help you to:
- understand the roles of trade unions and employers' associations in the employment relationship
- explain the objectives of trade unions and employers' associations
- identify the main trade unions and employers' associations in Ireland
- outline the typical structure of a trade union
- outline the functions of trade unions and employers' associations and the services they provide for their members

Introduction

This chapter examines the role of trade unions and employers' associations. You may remember the concept of **pluralism** from chapter one. This is the notion that workers and management have different objectives and need to protect their interests by showing a united front. Both trade unions and employers' associations represent groups of people protecting their own interests. Trade unions represent employees and employers' associations represent employers.

Trade Unions

Objectives of trade unions

According to Gunnigle *et al.* (2006, p.269), 'trade unions may be viewed as permanent associations of organised employees' whose primary objectives are to:
- replace individual bargaining with **collective bargaining**
- facilitate the development of a political system where workers' interests have a greater degree of influence on political decisions
- achieve satisfactory levels of **pay and conditions** of employment
- provide members with a range of services

Legal status

Every worker in Ireland has a constitutional right to be a member of a trade union. A worker who is a member of a trade union or involved in trade union activity is protected by laws such as the Unfair Dismissals Acts (1977–2007) and the Employment Equality Acts (1998–2008). However, organisations are not legally obliged to recognise any trade union and may refuse to negotiate with them.

For a group of workers to operate as a trade union, with a negotiating licence, there must be at least 1,000 members and a minimum deposit with the High Court of €25,395 (£20,000).

According to the Quarterly National Household Survey (Central Statistics Office, March 2010), 34 per cent of employees in Ireland are union members and full-time workers are more likely to join unions (37 per cent) than part-time workers (20 per cent).

Types of trade union

Gunnigle *et al.* (2006) group trade unions in Ireland into three broad categories, pointing out that nowadays it may be difficult to slot individual unions into one particular category:

- craft unions
- general unions
- white collar unions

Craft unions were the first unions to be established, in the mid-1800s. They represent skilled workers, such as carpenters, who had to serve an apprenticeship in their trade. At one time craft unions had a lot of power due to the fact that entry to the craft was controlled. In other words, only people who had completed a recognised apprenticeship and were union members were allowed to work in the trade. Because of technological developments in many areas of work, such as printing, the power of craft workers has decreased as their skills have become less valuable or even obsolete.

General unions have existed in Ireland since the 1860s but became more prominent in the early 1900s. The membership of general unions comprises workers from all occupations and industries. While traditionally general unions catered for unskilled or semi-skilled workers, nowadays they also attract craft and white collar workers too.

White collar unions mostly cater for professional, supervisory, clerical and managerial workers. There has been a big increase in membership since the 1960s and this can be partly attributed to the growth of the service sector in Ireland. White collar workers were not traditionally typical union members but may have been encouraged to become unionised by the success of general unions in improving pay and conditions for workers.

Today the Irish Congress of Trade Unions (ICTU) categorises unions under the following headings:

Table 9.1 *Trade union categories*

Type of trade union	Example
General unions	SIPTU (Services, Industrial, Professional and Technical Union)
Teachers' unions	TUI (Teachers' Union of Ireland)
Postal and telecommunications unions	CWU (Communications Workers' Union)
Other public service unions	IMPACT (Irish Municipal, Public and Civil Trade Union)
Electrical, engineering and construction unions	TEEU (Technical, Engineering and Electrical Union)
Other industry unions	Guinness Staff Union
Distribution, retail and transport unions	MANDATE
Professional and white collar unions	INO (Irish Nurses' Organisation)
Other unions	Association of Irish Traditional Musicians
Trades councils	Athlone Council of Trade Unions

Trade union structure

Figure 9.1 illustrates a typical trade union structure. The **shop steward** is an employee of the organisation who has been elected by co-workers to be the main trade union representative in the workplace, or in a particular section of the workplace. Shop stewards deal with employee grievances and inform members of union business, liaise with and support union officials and negotiate with management. Shop stewards are not paid for the work they do for the union but they are allowed a certain amount of time off work to carry out union duties.

A **union branch** is formed either by members from a number of smaller organisations or by members from one large organisation. The members of a branch are represented by a **branch committee**.

At national level, union officers are elected at the **annual delegates' conference**. A number of issues put forward by branches are discussed at the annual delegates' conference and this leads to the formulation of union policies. In this way decisions are made regarding the issues the union will focus on. The **general officers** of the union are usually full-time union employees.

Figure 9.1 *Example of trade union structure*

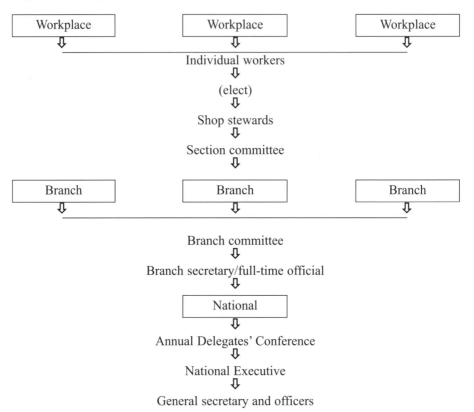

Irish Congress of Trade Unions (ICTU)

The Irish Congress of Trade Unions is the umbrella organisation for trade unions in Ireland. The main functions of ICTU are to:
- coordinate the work of trade unions in Ireland
- represent the interests of workers, especially to government
- assist with the resolution of disputes between unions and employers
- promote trade unionism and trade union policies
- negotiate national partnership agreements

ICTU is represented on government advisory bodies, and you will see in chapter ten that it nominates representatives for appointment to a number of bodies including the Labour Court and the Labour Relations Commission.

Alternatives to trade unions

It must be pointed out that workers have the right *not* to be a member of a trade union if they so choose. The alternatives to trade union membership are individual bargaining and staff associations.

Individual bargaining involves each employee negotiating on their own behalf and the outcomes of negotiating pay, conditions or any other matters apply only to the individual and not across the board, as is the case with the collective bargaining carried out by unions. Individual bargaining is most commonly used by highly skilled workers who feel they can do better by going it alone.

Staff associations are often formed by workers within an organisation as an alternative to trade unions. Membership is confined to workers within the organisation so, compared to the bigger trade unions, staff associations have limited bargaining power. Staff associations are traditionally associated with professional and managerial staff.

Employers' Associations

Services provided

Workers protect their interests by joining trade unions. Employers become members of employers' associations for similar reasons. Employers' associations provide services for their members similar to those provided by trade unions for their members. These services include:

- advising members on employment legislation and other matters relevant to human resource management
- carrying out research on, for example, economic trends and pay levels
- representing members in collective bargaining negotiations, at the Labour Court and at the Employment Appeals Tribunal
- representing members' views to the government, trade unions and the public
- providing training for members

Irish Business and Employers Confederation (IBEC)

IBEC is the largest employers' association in Ireland. It was established on 1 January 1993 as the result of a merger between the Federation of Irish Employers (FIE) and the Confederation of Irish Industry (CII). Today over 7,500 firms are members.

IBEC provides a wide range of services to individual member businesses and organisations from all sectors and of all sizes. Members have access to advice and expertise on employment legislation, HR best practice and health and safety. They can also avail of representation and negotiation on industrial relations/human resources issues. In addition, IBEC offers training and development and consultancy to members at a reduced rate. IBEC represents Irish business and employers both nationally and internationally.

Other employers' associations

Other employers' associations tend to be industry specific. Here are some examples:
- Construction Industry Federation (CIF)
- Irish Hotels Federation
- Society of the Irish Motor Industry (SIMI)
- Irish Pharmaceutical Union

Summary

Trade unions were discussed under the following headings:
- objectives
- legal status
- types
- structure
- ICTU
- alternatives

Employers' associations were discussed under these headings:
- services provided
- IBEC
- other employers' associations

Important Terms and Concepts

annual delegates' conference
branch committee
collective bargaining
craft unions
employers' association
general officers
general unions
IBEC
ICTU

individual bargaining
pay and conditions
shop steward
staff associations
trade union
union branch
union recognition
white collar unions

Revision Questions

1 Outline the role played by trade unions and employers' associations in employment relations.
2 Outline the structure of a typical trade union.
3 Compare the services provided to members of trade unions and members of employers' associations.

Further Information

The following websites provide excellent, detailed information which will supplement what you have learned in this chapter:

www.ibec.ie
www.ictu.ie
www.siptu.ie
www.sfa.ie
www.isme.ie

10
DISPUTE RESOLUTION

Objectives

This chapter will help you to:
- understand the voluntary nature of employment relations in Ireland
- recognise the importance of grievance and disciplinary procedures in preventing disputes
- identify the main state dispute-resolution facilities that exist
- understand the functions of the Labour Court, the Labour Relations Commission (LRC), the Employment Appeals Tribunal (EAT) and the Equality Tribunal
- understand the role of the National Employment Rights Authority (NERA) in the employment relationship

Introduction

In Ireland the primary responsibility for **employment relations** lies with management and unions. The system is **voluntary** in nature, which means that the government tends to stay out of negotiations and disputes as far as possible. With appropriate policies and procedures in place, most disputes can be solved without the need for third party intervention. The state has provided a number of agencies to deal with employment relations problems that cannot be resolved within the organisation.

Grievance and Disciplinary Procedures

When an employee is unhappy with something that management has done, or not done, as the case may be, this is called a **grievance**. Every organisation should have a **grievance procedure** in place so that employees know what steps they can take to have grievances addressed. Gunnigle *et al.* (2006) point out that the main aim of grievance procedures is to ensure that issues raised by employees are dealt with promptly and fairly, in order to avoid both the spread of dissent among workers and the escalation of the grievance into a serious industrial dispute.

When an employer is not satisfied with the work performance, behaviour or attitude of an employee, **disciplinary action** may be necessary. Every organisation should have a **disciplinary procedure** which informs employees of the consequences of not conforming to the rules and standards. These rules and standards must be clearly defined. Employers are obliged to inform workers of the disciplinary procedure.

Good grievance and disciplinary procedures are important so that cases can be dealt with fairly and consistently. Employee participation in the drawing up of these procedures is advised and increases the likelihood that the procedures will be accepted. The Labour Relations Commission provides guidelines for preparing codes of practice. Some important things to remember include:

- consider handling the matter on an informal basis first
- discuss the allegations or complaints with those concerned
- establish all the facts
- be objective
- allow the employee to be represented
- maintain a record at all stages of the procedure
- provide a right to appeal

Employers and employees are encouraged to sort out their differences themselves. However, the workload of the Labour Court and the Labour Relations Commission is increasing and organisations are being criticised for seeking third party intervention too easily. The next section examines the state facilities which exist to deal with employment relations problems that could not be solved in the workplace.

State Dispute-Resolution Facilities

1 The Labour Court
2 The Labour Relations Commission (LRC)
3 The Employment Appeals Tribunal (EAT)
4 The Equality Tribunal

1 The Labour Court

The Labour Court was established by the Industrial Relations Act (1946) and today provides a free service for resolving disputes about:

- industrial relations
- equality
- organisation of working time
- national minimum wage
- part-time work
- fixed-term work
- safety, health and welfare at work

Structure of the Labour Court

The Labour Court consists of nine full-time members: a chairman, two deputy chairmen and six ordinary members, three of whom are employers' members and three of whom are workers' members. The chairman and two deputy chairmen are appointed by the Minister for Enterprise, Trade and Innovation. The employers' members are nominated by IBEC and the workers' members are nominated by ICTU. A legal advisor (the registrar) is appointed by the Minister for Enterprise, Trade and Innovation.

The court operates in **three separate divisions** and each division is made up of either the chairman or a deputy chairman, one employers' member and one workers' member. Sometimes the full court may be required to deal with certain issues.

The process

The Labour Court is known as the **'court of last resort'**. This means that the parties involved should try to resolve the dispute within their organisation or else through the LRC or the rights commissioner service before coming to the Labour Court.

A case can arrive before the Labour Court in one of the following ways:
- referred by the LRC
- at the request of the Minister for Enterprise, Trade and Innovation
- to appeal the decision of a rights commissioner
- to appeal the decision of the Director of the Equality Tribunal
- directly to the Labour Court
- invitation from the Labour Court

Once a case has been correctly referred to the Labour Court, the parties involved will be allocated a date and venue as soon as possible. Cases are usually heard in Dublin, but the Labour Court also holds hearings at a number of venues around the country. Each party must supply the Court with written submissions stating their positions in relation to the dispute. During the hearing more information can be added to the written submission and members of the Court ask questions to clarify the situation. Hearings are usually held in private unless one of the parties requests that it should be held in public.

After the hearing the Labour Court will issue a written **recommendation** of how the dispute might be resolved, usually within three weeks. The Labour Court is not a court of law and its recommendations are generally not legally binding. The recommendation is offered as a third view and is expected to be considered seriously. An example of a case where the recommendation was not accepted was during the nurses' dispute in 2000. The Labour Court recommended that the nurses should accept the offer made to them, but the nurses opted to go on strike.

The Labour Court makes legally binding orders in cases where:

- employment legislation or registered employment agreements are breached
- the case is an appeal against the decision of a rights commissioner or an equality officer
- workers or unions agree to be bound by the Labour Court's recommendation

In addition, the Labour Court has new powers to issue binding recommendations on pay and conditions where union recognition does not exist.

In 2008 the Labour Court received 1,179 referrals and held 830 hearings at twenty locations around the country.

2 The Labour Relations Commission (LRC)

The LRC was set up in 1991 under the Industrial Relations Act (1990) to take over some of the responsibilities of the Labour Court. Its main functions are to:

- resolve disputes through its conciliation service
- provide an industrial relations advisory service to employers, workers and trade unions
- carry out and publish research on industrial relations
- provide a rights commissioner service
- prepare codes of practice and offer guidance on codes of practice
- provide a workplace mediation service

The main work of the LRC is its **conciliation service**. Conciliation is a voluntary mediation process and the parties involved in a dispute are encouraged to take responsibility for its resolution. An industrial relations officer (IRO) facilitates the resolution process by assisting the parties to find a mutually acceptable solution to their problems. The IRO first meets both parties together and then meets each party separately. A total of 1,571 disputes were referred to the conciliation service in 2009 (a 19 per cent increase over 2008) and settlements were reached in 82 per cent of cases.

The principal aim of the LRC's **advisory service** is to prevent industrial disputes from arising by helping employers and employees to build good relationships. It assists organisations in developing effective industrial relations practices, procedures and structures.

The LRC has responsibility for the **rights commissioner service** which operates as an independent service of the Commission. The rights commissioner service was originally the responsibility of the Labour Court but is now attached to the LRC. Rights commissioners are appointed by the Minister for Enterprise, Trade and Innovation. They investigate the disputes, grievances and claims of individuals or small groups of workers regarding areas of legislation such as unfair dismissal, payment of wages, maternity, young persons, holidays and minimum pay.

Investigations are conducted in private. The rights commissioner's recommendation or decision can be appealed to the Labour Court or the Employment Appeals Tribunal, depending on the type of dispute. In 2009, 14,569 cases were referred to the rights commissioner service, compared with 10,900 cases in 2008. Ninety per cent of the 2009 cases were taken by people who were not in employment when they made the claim. Cases in 2010 showed a continued increase, with 5,576 referrals for the first four months of that year.

The LRC has prepared the following **codes of practice**:
- procedures for addressing bullying in the workplace
- dispute procedures
- voluntary dispute resolution
- duties and responsibilities of employee representatives
- grievance and disciplinary procedures

These codes of practice are intended to give *guidance* to employers and trade unions on particular issues. They are not legally enforceable.

The **workplace mediation service**, which began in late 2005, is delivered as a separate service to the conciliation service. The service received 140 referrals in 2009. Issues included one-to-one interpersonal difficulties and group conflict. In the majority of these cases, the employer initiated the request for assistance.

3 The Employment Appeals Tribunal (EAT)

The EAT was established in 1967 and hears disputes in relation to legislation such as: unfair dismissal, redundancy payment, minimum notice, maternity protection, payment of wages, terms of employment, protection of young persons and part-time workers.

Structure of the EAT

The Tribunal consists of a chairman, forty-three vice-chairmen and eighty ordinary members from ICTU and employers' associations. It acts in divisions of three, the chairman or a vice-chairman as well as two ordinary members, one from ICTU and one from the employers' associations. Members of the EAT are appointed by the Minister for Enterprise, Trade and Innovation.

The process

Most cases have to go to the rights commissioner first, but cases regarding redundancy or minimum notice go directly to the EAT. Once an application to the EAT has been received by the Tribunal office, a copy of the application will be sent to the employer concerned. The employer will be asked to respond within fourteen days. It may be six months before a date for the hearing is decided and each party may bring witnesses to the hearing to give evidence on their behalf. The parties involved can represent themselves, or have a solicitor or a representative from their trade union or employers' association. The Tribunal is usually held in public but can be held in private in some situations. The Tribunal's determination is sent in writing a few weeks after the hearing.

In 2008, 5,457 cases were referred to the EAT and 4,007 were dealt with. Most of these cases related to unfair dismissal, minimum notice and terms of employment, and redundancy payment.

4 The Equality Tribunal

Established in 1999, the Equality Tribunal investigates and mediates claims of unlawful discrimination on the grounds of age, gender, family status, marital status, sexual orientation, disability, race, religion and membership of the Traveller community.

The investigation process

A claim of discrimination can be referred to the Equality Tribunal by an employee, a representative or the Equality Authority. An investigation is then carried out by a Tribunal equality officer. The decision of an equality officer is binding and enforceable by law. It is issued in writing after the hearing, normally contains full reasons and is required to be published. In employment cases, the Tribunal can award compensation of up to two years' pay. Decisions can be appealed to the Labour Court.

The mediation process

This alternative to the investigation process is carried out by an equality mediation officer. The process is voluntary and can be terminated by either party at any time. Mediation agreements are binding but confidential, so cannot be published. If there is no agreement, the investigation process may resume.

About 100 claims were made to the Equality Tribunal in 2000; that number had risen to 966 in 2009 and the majority of cases were on the grounds of gender, race and disability. The Tribunal awarded €617,500 in compensation in 2009, the average award was €12,350 and the highest award was €189,000. In 2009, 163 mediation sessions were held and 52 per cent of cases were resolved at the mediation table.

NERA

The National Employment Rights Authority (NERA) was established by the government in 2007 with the aim of achieving a national culture of employment rights compliance. NERA's main functions are to:
- provide free, unbiased **information** on employment rights in Ireland to employers, employees and other interested parties
- carry out both announced and unannounced **inspections** in organisations to check compliance with a range of employment legislation
- **enforce** compliance with employment legislation
- **prosecute** organisations for non-compliance with employment legislation in certain situations
- publish **codes of practice**

NERA inspected approximately 8,800 employers in 2009. The cases closed during this time showed a compliance rate of 69 per cent. These inspections resulted in the recovery of €2.5 million in unpaid wages for over 6,000 workers.

Summary

The employment relations system in Ireland is voluntary in nature. This means that employers and employees are usually expected to solve their own industrial disputes. When this proves too difficult, parties can make use of the services of the independent resolution facilities provided by the state. These are:
- The Labour Court
- The Labour Relations Commission

- The Employment Appeals Tribunal
- The Equality Tribunal

The main functions of NERA were outlined in this chapter.

Important Terms and Concepts

advisory, development and research service
conciliation service
disciplinary action
disciplinary procedure
dispute-resolution facilities
Employment Appeals Tribunal
employment relations
Equality Tribunal
grievance
grievance procedure
investigation process
Labour Court
Labour Relations Commission
mediation process
NERA
recommendation
rights commissioner service
voluntary
workplace mediation service

Revision Questions

1 Outline the state's involvement in employment relations in Ireland.
2 How can an organisation deal with its own employment relations problems?
3 Outline the functions of each of the following:
   (i)   The Labour Court
   (ii) The Labour Relations Commission
   (iii) The Employment Appeals Tribunal
   (iv) The Equality Tribunal
   (v)   NERA

Further Information

The following websites provide excellent, detailed information which will supplement what you have learned in this chapter:
   www.labourcourt.ie
   www.lrc.ie
   www.entemp.ie
   www.eatribunal.ie
   www.equalitytribunal.ie
   www.employmentrights.ie
   www.citizensinformation.ie/employment (also free guides in local offices)

11
EMPLOYMENT LEGISLATION

Objectives

This chapter will help you to:
- understand the role of employment legislation in the employer–employee relationship
- identify the obligations of employers towards their employees
- distinguish between a contract of service and a contract for service
- outline the laws regarding terms of employment, wages, dismissal, equality, maternity, health and safety, holidays, hours of work, young workers, minimum notice, part-time workers, fixed-term workers, minimum wage and pensions
- provide examples of relevant cases

Introduction

'The principal purpose of labour law is to regulate, to support and to restrain the power of management and the power of organised labour.' (Kahn-Freund, 1977) In other words, employment legislation provides a framework within which the worker–employer relationship can be managed. It is necessary for employers and managers to be familiar with current employment law in order to fulfil their legal obligations to their employees, and to be clear about their own rights, as well as those of their employees.

Employee Status

It is important to distinguish between a **contract of service** and a **contract for service**. An 'employee' is employed under a contract of service whereas an 'independent contractor' is employed under a contract for service. This distinction is important because only those under a contract of service have statutory protection, for example the right to claim unfair dismissal or maternity leave. Furthermore, employees under a contract of service get preference for payment when a company is winding up. The distinction between an employee and an independent contractor is often obvious, but not always. Problems can arise, for example, in situations regarding pension entitlements or redundancy payments.

The following questions are some of those considered by the courts when deciding the status of a particular worker:

- does the employer have the right to tell the individual *how* to carry out the work?
- is the individual integrated into, or part of, the employer's business?
- is the individual paid a wage/salary or a fee?
- are income tax and social insurance deducted by the organisation or by the individual?
- are tools and equipment provided by the organisation or by the individual?
- is the worker free to work for other organisations?

The National Employment Rights Authority (NERA) has co-authored a code of practice for determining the employment or self-employment status of individuals.

> Think of all the jobs you have done, including baby-sitting and weekend jobs. In each case do you think your status was that of an employee or an independent contractor?

The Contract of Employment

Relevant legislation: Terms of Employment (Information) Acts (1994 and 2001)

When a person is offered employment in return for wages, and accepts the offer, that is a contract of employment. The contract of employment does not have to be in writing but the Terms of Employment (Information) Act states that certain **terms of employment** must be available to the employee in writing within two months of taking up the post. This written statement must include:

- full names and addresses of employer and employee
- place of work
- job title or nature of work
- date of commencement of employment, duration of contract and expiry date if applicable
- details of pay and paid leave
- hours of work (including overtime) and details of rest breaks
- period of notice to be given by employer and employee

Some employers also include items such as rules and regulations, grievance procedures and disciplinary procedures. Employees may be referred to other documents, such as policy documents or the staff handbook, for additional information.

Employment legislation sets out the minimum rights to which an employee is entitled, such as minimum pay, minimum notice, holiday time and maternity leave. An employee's contract may provide for greater entitlements than the statutory minimum, but not less.

Procedure

The employee has the right to complain to a rights commissioner if the employer fails to provide a written statement in accordance with the Terms of Employment Act or fails to notify the employee of changes in the statement.

Wages

Relevant legislation: Payment of Wages Act (1991)
Employers are obliged to give each employee a written statement of gross wages itemising each deduction with every wage packet. Wages may be paid by cheque, credit transfer, cash, postal/money order or bank draft. Employers must not make deductions from wages unless required by law or with the written consent of the employee.

Procedure

Complaints may be referred to a rights commissioner.

Dismissal

Relevant legislation: Unfair Dismissals Acts (1977–2007)
                          Redundancy Payments Acts (1967–2007)
The purpose of the Unfair Dismissals Acts is to protect employees from being unfairly dismissed from their jobs. An employee who is dismissed from their employment can bring a claim for unfair dismissal against their employer once they have been in that employment for at least a year. The employee must have a contract *of* service.

Unfair dismissals

> Before you read this section, write down all the reasons you can think of where it would be unfair to dismiss an employee.

The Act states that a dismissal will be 'unfair' if it can be attributed to:
- trade union membership or activity
- religious or political opinion
- involvement in civil or criminal legal proceedings against the employer
- race or colour
- sexual orientation
- age
- unfair selection for redundancy
- taking maternity, adoptive, parental or carer's leave
- an employee exercising their right to a minimum wage
- being a member of the Travelling community
- pregnancy

The requirement to have one year's service does not apply if the dismissal can be attributed to one of the following:
- pregnancy or taking maternity leave, parental leave or adoptive leave
- an employee exercising their rights under the National Minimum Wage Act (2000)
- an employee taking carer's leave
- trade union membership or activity

Merriman v St James's Hospital (1986)

The plaintiff was dismissed because she refused, on religious grounds, to bring a crucifix and candle to a dying patient. The Circuit Court held that this was an unfair dismissal. The nurse was reinstated and was told by the judge that she had the right to be excused from participating in religious practices.

White v Simon Betson (1992)

The claimant maintained that although his weekly wage had been agreed when he started work, he was paid irregular amounts at regular intervals. He became a member of SIPTU, which wrote to the employer requesting a discussion on the employee's conditions of employment. He was dismissed after returning from sick leave. The Employment Appeals Tribunal found that he had been dismissed as a result of trade union membership.

Raouf Malek v Interactive Services (2003)

Mr Malek worked as a software tester for Interactive Services and achieved a score well above average in an appraisal test. The criteria that the firm had in place for making staff redundant were based on performance at the last employee appraisal review. The Employment Appeals Tribunal ruled that Mr Malek was unfairly selected for redundancy. He was awarded €12,000.

Maxwell v English Language Institute (1990)

A secretary submitted a maternity allowance claim form to her employer, who did not complete it. When she informed her employer that she was planning to take maternity leave, she was dismissed. The employer claimed that her work was unsatisfactory but the Employment Appeals Tribunal found that she had been dismissed because of her pregnancy.

Employees excluded from the Act

All employees are covered except those:
- with less than one year's continuous service
- over the normal retiring age
- employed by the Defence Forces and the Garda Síochána
- employed by the State
- employed by a close relative in a private house or farm where both parties live
- FÁS trainees and apprentices
- on probation at work

These exclusions from the Act do not apply where dismissal results from the employee's pregnancy or taking maternity leave, adoptive leave, parental leave or carer's leave.

In cases of unfair dismissal, the burden of proof usually lies with the employer. This means that, in general, every dismissal of an employee will be presumed to be unfair unless the employer can prove that the dismissal was justified.

Before you read the next section, think of possible situations where it would be appropriate for an employer to dismiss an employee.

Fair dismissal

Employers have the right to dismiss workers in certain circumstances. These can be discussed under the following headings:

- conduct
- capability
- competence
- qualifications
- redundancy

Conduct

An employee can be dismissed for conduct such as sick leave abuse, substance or alcohol abuse, dishonesty, criminal convictions, disobedience and violence. This can apply to off-duty conduct too.

Flynn v Sisters of Holy Faith (1985)

A secondary school teacher who had a baby with a man who was married to someone else was dismissed following complaints from parents. The case went to the EAT, the Circuit Court and the High Court and the teacher was found to have been fairly dismissed because her conduct violated her obligations to the school.

Hardy v Cadbury Ireland Ltd (1983)

The employee was found to be working for somebody else while out on sick leave. The EAT upheld the dismissal.

Capability

An employee can be dismissed if they do not have either the mental or the physical capability to do the job.

Guru v The Office of Public Works (1990)

The EAT found that there is no obligation on the employer to provide light work or alternative duties for an employee who is no longer capable of carrying out their duties.

Competence

An employee can be dismissed on the basis of competence. Poor work performance, substandard work and persistent lateness or absenteeism are justifiable reasons for dismissal.

Dixon v H Williams and Co Ltd (1981)

A shop assistant who was absent due to illness was found to be fairly dismissed, as attendance was poor over a period of time and appropriate warnings were given.

Qualifications

An employee can be dismissed if they do not have the qualifications necessary to do the job. An employee whose job description includes driving a vehicle could be dismissed if they lost their driver's licence.

Ryder and Byrne v Commissioners of Irish Lights (1980)

The employer required two members of staff to obtain higher technical qualifications within a reasonable time. The employees failed to comply with the requirement and were dismissed. The EAT upheld the dismissal.

Redundancy

An employee can be made redundant if the organisation is ceasing business or reducing its workforce. A worker may contest redundancy on the grounds of unfair selection for dismissal.

Redundancy payment According to the Redundancy Payments Acts (1967–2007) a worker employed by the organisation for two years is entitled to the following redundancy payment:
- two weeks' pay for each year in the employment
- plus one week's additional pay

Employers are entitled to a rebate of 60 per cent from the Department of Enterprise, Trade and Innovation, provided they have given the employee two weeks' notice and have paid the statutory redundancy.

Constructive dismissal

An employee who leaves a job, rather than being dismissed, may still have a claim for unfair dismissal. Constructive dismissal occurs when an employee leaves the workplace but is treated as having been dismissed because the employer's conduct has made it impossible for the employee to stay. In this case the burden of proof lies with the employee.

Liz Allen v Independent Newspapers (2001)

Liz Allen was a crime correspondent with the *Sunday Independent* newspaper. She took a case of constructive dismissal against her employers, Independent Newspapers, because the treatment she received from some of her colleagues forced her to leave. She felt she had no option but to resign because she had been isolated and bullied at work and her confidence and health had been undermined. She won her case and was awarded over £70,000 (€88,882) in compensation. The EAT made the award on the basis that the defendants had not taken action on her complaints made over a two-year period.

Procedure

An unfair dismissals case can be brought to a rights commissioner or the EAT within six months of dismissal, or twelve months in exceptional circumstances. Either party may appeal the Tribunal's decision to the Circuit Court within six weeks.

Employers' obligations

When a case is taken to the EAT, the Tribunal will try to assess whether the employer dealt with the situation in a reasonable manner.

The Unfair Dismissals Acts (1977–2007) require employers to give notice in writing to each employee explaining the organisation's dismissal procedure. This information must be given within twenty-eight days of entering into a contract of employment.

Fennell and Lynch (1993) have identified four basic obligations of employers with regard to the procedures involved in dismissing an employee. These are:

- **investigation** – the employer needs to show that the matter was investigated fairly before a decision was made to dismiss the individual

- **hearing** – the employee must be given an opportunity to respond and should be allowed to have trade union representation at this meeting
- **warning** – as far as possible, the employee should be given a warning and an opportunity to improve
- **proportionate penalties** – the Tribunal decides whether dismissal was fair and in proportion to the behaviour of the employee

---

A Worker v Dejay Royale (2004)

The worker was dismissed for poor performance but had received no warning, either verbal or written, at any stage prior to being dismissed. The Labour Court found that the company's disciplinary procedures were inappropriate and awarded the claimant €20,000 in compensation.

Unfair dismissal remedies

The EAT may decide an employee was unfairly dismissed but must assess to what extent each party was at fault. This decision affects the remedy chosen.

Reinstatement is the return of the employee to their previous job with back pay. It is effectively as if the dismissal never took place and the employee must benefit from any improvement in terms and conditions of employment which may have occurred between the date of dismissal and the date of reinstatement.

Re-engagement allows the employee to return to their previous job or a similar job, usually without back pay.

Compensation is the most common remedy and has a maximum of 104 weeks' pay. It may be given in addition to the other remedies or on its own. An employee found to have been unfairly dismissed but who has suffered no financial loss may be awarded up to four weeks' pay.

In 2008 the EAT ordered seven reinstatements and four re-engagements and nearly €3 million was paid out in compensation, an average of €11,476 per case.

Employment Equality

Relevant legislation: Employment Equality Acts (1998–2008)
This legislation protects employees against discrimination at work on nine distinct grounds:
- gender
- marital status

- family status
- sexual orientation
- religious belief
- age
- disability
- race
- membership of the Travelling community

Employees are protected from discrimination with regard to recruitment advertising, employment, conditions of employment, training and promotion.

Freeman v Superquinn (2002)

In March 2002, Superquinn was ordered to pay €20,000 in compensation to an employee at one of its Dublin stores who was discriminated against on the grounds of age, marital status and family status when she applied for the post of head cashier. It was the first case to be won on the marital status and family status grounds under the Employment Equality Act (1998).

Dr Bennet Eng v St James's Hospital (2002)

In December 2001, the Office of the Director of Equality Investigations (now The Equality Tribunal) found that St James's Hospital discriminated against Dr Bennet Eng on racial grounds. It was found to be unlawful for Dr Eng to work as an intern without a basic salary when his Irish colleagues working beside him were in salaried positions. The case was appealed to the Labour Court in May 2002 and the decision of the equality officer was upheld.

Gleeson v Rotunda and Mater Hospitals (2000)

In this case of gender discrimination, Dr Noreen Gleeson was awarded £50,000 (€63,500). When she was being interviewed for a job, she was asked about the time she 'had her babies'. The Labour Court found that Dr Gleeson was better qualified, more experienced and better published than the successful male applicant.

Hughes v Aer Lingus (2002)

The claimant felt that she had been discriminated against because of her age, she was fifty-three, when she was turned down for a cabin crew position. She was asked how she would cope with younger people being in charge and how, being older, she would feel about starting at the bottom rung of the ladder. The equality officer found that the complainant's age was not the reason that her application was unsuccessful, as three candidates over the age of fifty had been offered positions. However, the equality officer found that Ms Hughes had been discriminated against on the ground of her age in the manner in which she was questioned at interview. The claimant was awarded €5,000 and Aer Lingus was ordered to offer her another interview within twelve weeks, or offer her a cabin crew position.

A Worker v A Company (2002)

A claimant with cerebral palsy was asked to carry out tasks that she found difficult due to her disability. She left her job and contended that she had been constructively dismissed. She was awarded €9,000 when the Labour Court found that her employer had not done 'all that is reasonable to accommodate the needs of a person with a disability'.

A Worker v A Company (2005)

The Labour Court awarded almost €60,000 to a man it found was discriminated against because of a psychiatric illness. The man had been hospitalised from April to June 2002 but his employer did not allow him to return to work until October. He was told that he could no longer deal with clients and that his work would be monitored. The man then resigned because he felt he was not wanted at work.

Maguire v NE Health Board (2002)

The equality officer found that a temporary care attendant was treated differently by staff and management when they discovered that he was a Traveller. The equality officer also found that management had failed in its obligations to investigate the complaint. The NE Health Board was ordered to implement a harassment policy and to pay the claimant €5,000 for stress suffered.

A Health Service Employee v Health Service Executive (2006)

A care assistant was offered the post of staff nurse in a temporary capacity subject to Occupational Health clearance. She was frequently deployed as a staff nurse during times of short staffing. The Occupational Health nurse told the claimant that she was morbidly obese and that she could not be accepted as a nurse. The Occupational Health physician suggested that she would have difficulty in accessing patients because of her weight and that she would not be able to run fast enough if there was an emergency. It was suggested that she have her stomach stapled. The claimant's position was deferred for six months but she was subsequently employed on a permanent contract. An equality officer found that the claimant had been discriminated against on the ground of disability and awarded her compensation of €3,000 as well as back pay.

Meehan v Leitrim County Council (2006)

The Equality Tribunal found that a fireman was discriminated against on the ground of age in relation to promotion. The claimant had better qualifications and experience than the successful candidate. He was awarded €5,000 in compensation and Leitrim County Council was ordered to ensure that all aspects of their interview processes are transparent and free from discrimination and that all interview notes are retained.

Czerski v ICE Group (2006)

A Polish woman was awarded €7,000 in compensation after the Equality Tribunal found that she had been indirectly discriminated against on the ground of race. She had been unable to provide two work-related references to the employment agency.

O'Neill v Board of Management, St Gabriel's National School (2005)

At an interview a teacher was asked 'considering that you have been teaching for 27 years, why would you now be bothered with the hassle of the job of Deputy Principal?'. The equality officer found that the teacher was discriminated against on the ground of age and awarded €5,000 in compensation.

An Employee v A Government Department (2005)

An employee claimed that he was not selected for promotion because he was an alcoholic. He had been in recovery since receiving treatment in 1995. The equality officer found that the claimant had been discriminated against on the ground of disability and ordered that he be appointed to the relevant grade with immediate effect and that he receive back pay and benefits. The claimant was also awarded €6,000 in compensation.

Connolly v Bons Secour Hospital (2005)

A part-time porter who had worked at the hospital for over eight years applied for one of two positions for full-time night porter. He was unsuccessful in his application and was told that the reason for this was that he was married with children. The equality officer found that this was not the reason that the claimant was unsuccessful in his application because one of the successful applicants was married with a child. However, the claimant was awarded €6,000 as compensation for the discriminatory comment made at the feedback discussion.

Mr M v A Language School, Dublin (2004)

A man complained that he was discriminated against on the ground of gender when an offer of appointment as manager of the school was withdrawn. The school was operated by a religious community. It was felt that the job was unsuitable for a man as it involved visiting host families and 'dealing with the lady of the house' and with homesick or emotional Italian students. The complainant was awarded €12,697 in compensation for gender discrimination.

Piazza v The Clarion Hotel (2004)

An employee was awarded €10,000 in compensation when an equality officer found that he had been discriminated against on the ground of sexual orientation on three occasions. It was found that an investigation undertaken by management in response to complaints was unsatisfactory. The hotel was ordered to revise and redraft its Respect and Dignity document and to provide equality training to all staff including management within three months.

Ms A v A Contract Cleaning Company (2004)

Ms A was employed as a cleaner at a shopping centre in the Midlands. She claimed that she had been sexually harassed by a security guard who worked at the shopping centre but was employed by a security firm. Ms A claimed that the security guard had made crude and sexually offensive remarks to her and her colleagues on several occasions, and these incidents were reported to management. Then, on one particular occasion, the security guard pushed Ms A into the staff canteen and, in front of her supervisor, pulled down her trousers and underwear and smacked her on the bare bottom, laughed out loud and left the room. When she raised the incident with her supervisor, the supervisor said it was only a joke. Ms A reported the incident to the Gardaí but withdrew her statement when her employer told her she would lose her job if she did not. The equality officer found that Ms A had been discriminated against on the ground of gender and ordered that she be paid the maximum amount in compensation, i.e. two years' wages. This amounted to €21,000 and the equality officer stated that if she could have ordered a significantly higher award, she would have done so. The company was ordered to review its sexual harassment policy and to organise training for staff.

Procedure

Complaints may be directed to the Equality Tribunal within six months.

Maternity Leave

Relevant legislation: Maternity Protection Acts (1994–2004)
This legislation sets out the main entitlements and obligations of pregnant employees:

- all employees are covered regardless of period of service or number of hours worked per week
- the employee is allowed to attend certain ante- and post-natal medical visits without loss of pay
- since March 2007 the employee is entitled to twenty-six weeks' paid leave, two of which must be taken before the birth and four after
- maternity benefit of up to 70 per cent of income is paid by the Department of Social Protection (some organisations supplement the maternity benefit)
- the employee may take up to sixteen weeks' unpaid leave
- the employee must give four weeks' notice before going on maternity leave as well as presenting a medical certificate
- the employee must notify the organisation in writing at least four weeks in advance of her return

Procedure

Disputes concerning any of the above entitlements may be referred to a rights commissioner within six months.

Health and Safety

Relevant legislation: Safety, Health and Welfare at Work Acts (1989 and 2005) Safety, Health and Welfare at Work (General Application) Regulations (1993)
According to this legislation employers are primarily responsible for creating and maintaining a safe and healthy workplace. Every employer must provide a safe workplace and is required to prepare a safety statement for the workplace. This statement should identify any hazards that exist and outline the measures that are to be taken to deal with these risks.

Employees too are responsible for health and safety at work and must be consulted on any matters dealing with health and safety in the workplace. Employees are obliged to wear protective equipment when necessary and to take care when using machinery, tools and substances.

According to the Health and Safety Authority's annual report, 43 people died as a result of work-related accidents in 2009, the lowest number of fatalities since the HSA was formed. Most fatal accidents were due to loss of control of means of transport or handling equipment and falling from a height. The majority of deaths occurred in the farming and construction sectors. The number of non-fatal serious accidents notified formally to the Authority in 2008 was 17,900. The Authority concluded thirty-eight prosecutions resulting in those convicted being fined a total of €708,850.

Smurfit News Press Ltd (2004)

Smurfit News Press Ltd was fined €1 million for health and safety violations at a plant in Kells following an investigation by the Health and Safety Authority into two serious accidents. In the first incident, the employee was working at a printing press when his leg became trapped and subsequently had to be amputated below the knee. Two weeks later another employee at the same plant seriously injured his hand when it became trapped in a printing press. The court was informed that the cause of the accidents was inadequate guarding and a failure to prepare an adequate risk assessment on the hazards involved in working on the printing presses.

Oran Pre-Cast Concrete Ltd (2003)

In July 2003, Oran Pre-Cast Concrete was fined €500,000 for breaches of health and safety legislation. The conviction followed an investigation by the Health and Safety Authority into the death of a 25-year-old man in an accident at work. The employee fell from a height of nine metres while replacing a damaged roof gutter on a building. The man who died had not received adequate safety training for the height at which he was working when the accident happened. The fine was reduced to €100,000 on appeal.

Early Learning Centre (2003)

In January 2003, the Early Learning Centre store in Galway was fined €600 for breaches of health and safety legislation. Staff members had not received adequate training or instruction in manual handling. In addition, the company did not have a safety statement for its Eyre Square store as required under health and safety legislation.

Kilkishen Homes (2003)

In January 2003, a director of Kilkishen Homes was jailed for three days for contempt of court after he failed to comply with an undertaking to provide scaffolding for workers building houses. The court also fined the company €10,000.

Roadstone Dublin Ltd (2003)

In February 2003, Roadstone Dublin Ltd was fined €12,000 following a serious accident that resulted in an employee's left hand being amputated. The employee had been carrying out maintenance on machinery. Costs and expenses were awarded to the Health and Safety Authority.

Tara Mines Ltd (2002)

In November 2002, Tara Mines Ltd was fined €3,808 for breaches of health and safety legislation following an accident where an employee lost his right eye. The company had failed to include an assessment of the risks associated with a particular machine in its safety statement. Costs were awarded to the Health and Safety Authority.

Inchagoill Contractors Ltd, K9 Securities (2001)

An 18-year-old security man was accidentally poisoned by carbon monoxide on his first night at work. He died in an upstairs bedroom of a newly constructed house. A petrol-driven generator on the ground floor had been providing power for a TV set in the bedroom. Inchagoill Contractors Ltd was fined €3,000 for failing to ensure that the workplace was safe. K9 Securities was fined €250 for failing to secure the health, safety and welfare of the deceased in connection with the use of a petrol-driven generator.

Bantry Hospital (1998)

A nurse who suffered a serious back injury while lifting patients was awarded damages of £159,046 (€201,947) by the High Court but had the reward reduced by one-third to £106,031 (€134,632) as a result of what the judge declared was her own contributory negligence. The nurse had instructed the assistant in what to do but did not reprimand her when she failed to lift in the correct way.

Procedure

For issues regarding health and safety, contact the Health and Safety Authority.

Holidays

Relevant legislation: Organisation of Working Time Act (1997)

Annual leave

- all employees are entitled to at least twenty days' annual leave
- all employees are entitled to an unbroken period of two weeks' annual leave once they have worked for eight months
- holiday pay can be calculated as 8 per cent of hours worked in a leave year
- calculation of holidays should include overtime, time spent on annual leave, maternity leave, parental leave, force majeure leave, adoptive leave and time spent on the first thirteen weeks of carer's leave
- part-time, temporary and casual employees are entitled to 8 per cent of hours worked
- holiday pay is paid in advance at the normal weekly rate
- a day of sickness during holidays which is covered by a medical certificate is not counted as annual leave

Public holidays

- employees are entitled to nine public holidays every year (Christmas Day, St Stephen's Day, New Year's Day, St Patrick's Day, Easter Monday, the first Mondays in May, June and August, the last Monday in October) and the employer must provide one of the following:
  - a paid day off on the public holiday
  - a paid day off within a month of the public holiday

- a specified Church holiday falling immediately before or after the public holiday in lieu
- an additional day of annual leave
- an additional day's pay if an employee works on the public holiday
- the employer must inform the employee which of these alternatives will apply at least two weeks before the public holiday takes place
- there is no service requirement in respect of public holidays for full-time employees
- part-time employees are only entitled to a public holiday if they have worked at least forty hours during the five weeks immediately prior to the public holiday
- if the public holiday falls on a day on which the employee does not normally work, the employee is entitled to one-fifth of their normal weekly wage for the day, a paid day off within a month or an extra day's annual leave

When an employee leaves the organisation, they are entitled to be paid any holiday leave due to them either in the current year or in the previous one. The employer must keep records of holidays and public holidays for at least three years to show that the Act is being complied with.

Zevas Communications Ltd and A Worker (2005)

The claimant was employed by the respondent from August to October 2003. He claimed that he did not receive holiday pay of €35.31 and payment for a bank holiday of €49.53. The rights commissioner awarded the employee €84.80 and this decision was upheld by the Labour Court.

Gerry Kelly Enterprises Ltd and Andris Reinfelds (2002)

In 2002, a bricklayer who was not paid for public holidays or annual leave to which he was entitled was awarded €345 compensation for loss of holiday pay and €1,000 additional compensation.

> ## Prime News Ltd and L. Patchell (2002)
>
> The Labour Court determined that Ms Patchell, a part-time worker, should be paid a total of €1,376.56 in respect of unpaid annual leave and public holiday entitlement.

Procedure

Complaints in relation to holiday entitlements may be directed to a rights commissioner within six months of the dispute occurring.

For details of these and other Labour Court cases see the Labour Court website.

Hours of Work and Rest Breaks

Relevant legislation: Organisation of Working Time Act (1997)

Maximum weekly working time

The maximum average working week is forty-eight hours. Averaging may be balanced out over a four-, six- or twelve-month period depending on the circumstances.

Zero hours

When an employee is requested to be available for work but then is not needed, they are entitled to be paid for either 25 per cent of the time that they were required to be available or fifteen hours, whichever is less. For example, if an employee is asked to be available to work eight hours and is not called in to work, the employee will be entitled to a minimum payment of two hours. An employee must be informed at least twenty-four hours in advance of starting and finishing times or any other changes in working times.

Rest breaks

Every employee has a general entitlement to:
- a daily rest break of eleven consecutive hours
- fifteen minutes where more than four-and-a-half hours have been worked
- thirty minutes where more than six hours have been worked, which may include the first break

- shop employees whose hours of work include the hours 11.30 am to 2.30 pm must be allowed a break of one hour after six hours' work commencing between the hours of 11.30 am and 2.30 pm
- night workers whose work involves special hazards or a heavy physical or mental strain can work a maximum of eight hours in a twenty-four hour period

Procedure

Complaints may be directed to a rights commissioner.

Young Workers

Relevant legislation: Protection of Young Persons (Employment) Act (1996)

- children over fourteen can do light work outside school term for no more than seven hours in any day or thirty-five hours in any week
- children over fifteen, but under sixteen, may work up to eight hours a week doing light work during school term time
- children under sixteen may not work between 8 pm and 8 am
- young persons, i.e. between the ages of sixteen and eighteen, may work for a maximum of eight hours in one day or forty hours in one week
- young persons may not be employed between the hours of 10 pm and 6 am
- the employer is obliged to see the birth certificate of employees under eighteen and to get written permission from the parents or guardian of employees under sixteen
- employers who employ young people under the age of eighteen must give a summary of the Act to the employee

---

Smyth's Pub Malahide (2005)

At Dublin District Court a publican was fined €66,500 for thirty-five breaches of child worker legislation. In one case a fifteen-year-old girl worked until 1.30 am, five-and-a-half hours after she should have finished work. Other cases involved sixteen- and seventeen-year-olds working until 2 am.

Portmarnock Hotel and Golf Links (2005)

This case involved two boys, aged sixteen and seventeen, who had worked for a number of hours later than the 10 pm limit, up to 3 am in one case. Fines totalling €18,000 were imposed at Dublin District Court.

Supermac's (2003)

In February 2003, the Loughrea branch of Supermac's fast-food restaurant was fined €3,400 for allowing two seventeen-year-old students to work after 10 pm.

Procedure

Complaints may be directed to a rights commissioner.

Minimum Notice

Relevant legislation: **Minimum Notice and Terms of Employment Acts (1973–2005)**

Once an employee has worked for thirteen weeks in a job, they are entitled to notice before the employer may dismiss them. The minimum notice provided for is displayed in table 11.1.

Table 11.1 *Minimum notice*

Duration of employment	Minimum notice
13 weeks to 2 years	1 week
2 years to 5 years	2 weeks
5 years to 10 years	4 weeks
10 years to 15 years	6 weeks
15 years or more	8 weeks

The Act requires an employee to give an employer one week's notice of leaving once they have been in that employment for thirteen weeks. However, a contract of employment may provide for a greater period of notice to be given by the employee.

Procedure

Disputes concerning minimum notice may be referred to the Employment Appeals Tribunal.

Part-time Workers

Relevant legislation: Protection of Employees (Part-Time Work) Act (2001)

This Act came into effect on 20 December 2001 and specifies that part-time workers cannot be treated any less favourably than a 'comparable' full-time employee when it comes to their conditions of employment such as pay, pension, holidays, voluntary health contributions and entitlement to sick pay. Part-time workers who work at least 20 per cent of the normal hours of the comparable full-time employee are entitled to any pension schemes or arrangements that are enjoyed by full-time employees.

Dunnes Stores Letterkenny and SIPTU (2005)

Part-time employees claimed that they received less favourable treatment than full-time employees as regards the sick pay scheme. The rights commissioner ordered the employer to treat the claimants no less favourably in respect of sick pay than the named comparable full-time employee. The Labour Court awarded the claimants €500 each.

Procedure

Disputes concerning part-time workers' legislation may be referred to a rights commissioner.

Fixed-term Workers

Relevant legislation: Protection of Employees (Fixed-Term Work) Act (2003)

This legislation stipulates that employees on fixed-term contracts must not be treated less favourably than comparable permanent workers. In addition, employers cannot repeatedly renew fixed-term contracts. Under this Act employees can only work on one or more fixed-term contracts for a continuous period of four years. After this, the employee is entitled to a contract of indefinite duration (CID).

Marian College and Aisling Russell (2008)

The complainant commenced employment as a teacher in September 2001. She requested a CID in September 2005 but was instead given another fixed-term contract. In February 2006 she was offered a CID but she refused it on the grounds that the terms of the contract were less favourable than for comparable employees. The Labour Court determined that the complainant was deemed to have a CID from September 2005 and that the terms and conditions must be the same as those of a comparable permanent employee. In addition, the complainant was awarded compensation of €3,000.

Minimum Wage

Relevant legislation: National Minimum Wage Act (2000)

In April 2000 the national minimum wage came into effect. At that time employees, with some exceptions, were guaranteed a minimum wage of €5.59 per hour. There is a provision in the legislation for this figure to be reviewed at regular intervals and already there have been several increases. The minimum wage was raised to €8.65 per hour in July 2007.

Employees under the age of eighteen are guaranteed up to 70 per cent of the national minimum wage. In the first year after reaching eighteen years of age, 80 per cent of the national minimum wage is guaranteed; in the second year, 90 per cent; and in the third year, 100 per cent. This also applies to over-eighteens who enter employment for the first time.

Certain employees who are over eighteen and undergoing a course of training or study authorised by the employer are only guaranteed a reduced national minimum wage.

Zevas Communications Ltd and A Worker (2005)

The claimant was employed by the respondent from August to October 2003. He claimed that during that period he was paid €5.29 per hour compared to the minimum wage of €6.36 and claimed arrears of €441.44 plus expenses. The respondent denied the claim, saying that the claimant worked twenty-five hours per week and was paid €6.71 per hour while training for the first month and €8.00 per hour thereafter. The respondent did not produce any records at the hearing. The rights commissioner awarded €441.44 in arrears and €60 expenses.

Ivory Hotel v Rita Gedminaite (2002)

In a case against the Ivory Hotel in Waterford, a claimant was awarded €1,047 arrears of wages under the National Minimum Wage Act (2000).

Procedure

The employee may request an inspector from the Department of Enterprise, Trade and Innovation to investigate a claim that the national minimum wage is not being paid.

Pensions

Relevant legislation: Pensions (Amendment) Act (2002)
Since September 2003 all employers in Ireland are obliged to provide access to at least one standard personal retirement savings account (PRSA) for their employees. This means that employers must provide the facility to deduct contributions from an employee's pay and transfer it to a pension plan if that employee wishes to be part of a pension scheme. The employer can choose the PRSA provider(s) but does not have to contribute to the PRSA on behalf of an employee.

Procedure

Complaints may be directed to the Pensions Ombudsman.

Summary

The main aspects of employment legislation covered in this chapter were:
- the distinction between a contract *of* service and a contract *for* service
- wages
- dismissal
- employment equality
- maternity leave
- health and safety
- holidays, hours of work and rest breaks
- young workers
- minimum notice
- part-time workers
- fixed-term workers
- minimum wage
- pensions

Table 11.2 *Summary of principal employment legislation*

Terms of Employment (Information) Acts (1994 and 2001)
Payment of Wages Act (1991)
Unfair Dismissals Acts (1977–2007)
Redundancy Payments Acts (1967–2007)
Employment Equality Acts (1998–2008)
Maternity Protection Acts (1994–2004)
Safety, Health and Welfare at Work Acts (1989 and 2005)
Safety, Health and Welfare at Work (General Application) Regulations (1993)
Organisation of Working Time Act (1997)
Protection of Young Persons (Employment) Act (1996)
Minimum Notice and Terms of Employment Acts (1973–2005)
Protection of Employees (Part-Time Work) Act (2001)
Protection of Employees (Fixed-Term Work) Act (2003)
National Minimum Wage Act (2000)
Pensions (Amendment) Act (2002)

Important Terms and Concepts

annual leave
capability
compensation
competence
conduct
constructive dismissal
contract for service
contract of employment
contract of service
Employment Appeals Tribunal
employment equality
fair dismissal
fixed-term workers
health and safety
hearing
holidays
hours of work
investigation
maternity leave

minimum notice
minimum wage
part-time workers
payment of wages
pensions
proportionate penalties
public holidays
qualifications
redundancy
re-engagement
reinstatement
rest breaks
rights commissioner
terms of employment
unfair dismissal
warning
young workers
zero hours

Revision Questions

1 Distinguish between a contract of service and a contract for service. Why is this distinction important?
2 When is dismissal deemed to be 'unfair'?
3 What are the basic obligations of the employer with regard to dismissal?
4 When is it 'fair' for an employer to dismiss an employee?
5 Explain what is meant by 'constructive dismissal'.
6 Outline the remedies for unfair dismissal.
7 Outline the main aspects of maternity legislation.
8 Outline the holiday entitlements of employees.

Further Information

The following websites provide excellent, detailed information which will supplement what you have learned in this chapter:

www.employmentrights.ie
www.entemp.ie
www.labourcourt.ie
www.eatribunal.ie
www.citizensinformation.ie
www.hsa.ie
www.equalitytribunal.ie

Explanatory booklets relevant to the content of this chapter are available, free of charge, from **Citizens' Information Centres**.

REFERENCES

Adams, J. S. (1963), 'Towards an understanding of inequity', *Journal of Abnormal and Social Psychology*, November, pp.422–36.

Alderfer, C. P. (1972), *Existence, Relatedness and Growth*, New York: Free Press.

Armstrong, M. (1993), *A Handbook of Personnel Management Practice*, London: Kogan Page.

Armstrong, M. (1999), *A Handbook of Human Resource Management Practice*, 7th edition, London: Kogan Page.

Armstrong, M. (2001), *A Handbook of Human Resource Management Practice*, 8th edition, London: Kogan Page.

Armstrong, M. (2006), *A Handbook of Human Resource Management Practice*, 10th edition, London: Kogan Page.

Armstrong, M. (2009), *Armstrong's Handbook of Human Resource Management Practice*, 11th edition, London: Kogan Page.

Beardwell, J. and Claydon, T. (2007), *Human Resource Management: A Contemporary Approach*, 5th edition, Harlow: Prentice Hall.

Beardwell, I. and Holden, L. (1997), *Human Resource Management: A Contemporary Perspective*, London: Pitman.

Benge, E. (1944), *Job Evaluation and Merit Rating*, Washington: US National Foreman's Institute.

Central Statistics Office (March 2010), *Quarterly National Household Survey*, Dublin: CSO.

CIPD (2009), *Promoting the Value of Learning in Adversity*, London: Chartered Institute of Personnel and Development.

CIPD (2009), *Recruitment, Retention and Turnover*, London: Chartered Institute of Personnel and Development.

CIPD (2010), *Resourcing and Talent Planning*, London: Chartered Institute of Personnel and Development.

Fennel, C. and Lynch, I. (1993), *Labour Law in Ireland*, Dublin: Gill & Macmillan.

Foot, M. and Hook, C. (2008), *Introducing Human Resource Management*, 5th edition, Harlow: Financial Times Prentice Hall.

Gibb, S. and Megginson, D. (1993), 'Inside corporate mentoring schemes – a new agenda of concerns', *Personnel Review*, Vol.22, No.1, pp.40–54.

Guest, D. (1989), 'Personnel and HRM: Can you tell the difference?', *Personnel Management*, January.

Guest, D. (1997), 'Human resource management and performance: A review and research agenda', *International Journal of Human Resource Management*, Vol.8, No.3, pp.263–76.

Gunnigle, P. and Flood, P. (1990), *Personnel Management in Ireland*, Dublin: Gill & Macmillan.

Gunnigle, P., Heraty, N. and Morley, M. (1997), *Personnel and Human Resource Management: Theory and Practice in Ireland*, Dublin: Gill & Macmillan.

Gunnigle, P., Heraty, N. and Morley, M. (2006), *Human Resource Management in Ireland*, Dublin: Gill & Macmillan.

Heery, E. and Noon, M. (2001), *A Dictionary of Human Resource Management*, Oxford University Press.

Herzberg, F. (1966), *Work and the Nature of Man*, Cleveland: World Publishing Company.

Hill, J. and Trist, E. (1955), 'Changes in accidents and other absences with length of service', *Human Relations*, 8 May.

Kahn-Freund, O. (1977), *Labour and the Law*, London: Stevens.

Kirkpatrick, D. L. (1959, 1960), 'Techniques for evaluating training', *Journal of the American Society of Training Directors,* Vol.13, pp.3–9, 21–26; Vol.14, pp.13–18, 28–32.

Kotter, J. P. and Schlesinger, L. A. (1979), 'Choosing strategies for change', *Harvard Business Review*. Reprinted in 2008 and available at http://government.hbsp.org/corporate/assets/content/ChoosingStrategies.pdf (last accessed August 2010).

Latham, G. P. and Wexley, K. N. (1981), *Increasing Productivity through Performance Appraisal*, Wokingham: Addison-Wesley.

Lawler, E. (1977), 'Reward systems', in J. Hackman and J. Suttle (eds.), *Improving Life at Work: Behavioural Science Approaches to Organisational Change*, pp. 163–226, New York: Goodyear.

Maslow, A. H. (1943), 'A theory of human motivation', *Psychological Review*, No.50, July, pp.370–96.

McClelland, D. (1961), *The Achieving Society*, Princeton, NJ: Van Nostrand.

McGregor, D. (1960), *The Human Side of Enterprise*, New York: McGraw-Hill.

Muchinsky, P. (1986), 'Personnel selection methods', in C. Cooper and I. Robertson (eds.), *International Review of Industrial and Organizational Psychology*, pp.37–70, New York: Wiley.

Pettinger, R. (1994), *Introduction to Management*, London: Macmillan.

Pfeffer, J. (1998), *The Human Equation*, Boston, MA: Harvard Business School.

Porter, M. E. (1985), *Competitive Advantage*, New York: Free Press.

Reilly, R. and Chao, G. (1982), 'Validity and fairness of some alternative employee selection procedures', *Personnel Psychology*, No.35, pp.1–62.

Roberts, G. (1997), *Recruitment and Selection: A Competency Approach*, London: Institute of Personnel and Development.

Rodger, A. (1952), *The Seven-Point Plan*, London: National Institute of Industrial Psychology.

Rogers, C. R. (1947), 'Some observations on the organisation of personality', *American Psychologist*, Vol.2, pp.358–68.

Small Firms Association (2007), '340,000 Irish workers moved jobs in 2007!', press release, Dublin: SFA.

Steers, R. M. and Porter, L. W. (eds.) (1991), *Motivation and Work Behaviour*, 5th edition, New York: McGraw-Hill.